W9-CAY-761

Eastbluff Homeowners
Community Association

ANGELS ESSENTIAL

Everything You Need to Know to Be a Real Fan!

Steven Travers

TRIUMPH
BOOKS

Library of Congress Cataloging-in-Publication Data

Travers, Steven.
    Angels essential : everything you need to know to be a real fan! / Steven Travers.
        p. cm.
    Includes bibliographical references.
    ISBN-13: 978-1-57243-943-6
    ISBN-10: 1-57243-943-2
        1. Los Angeles Angels of Anaheim (Baseball team)—History.
    2. Baseball—California—Los Angeles—History.   I. Title.

GV875.L6T73 2007
796.357'640979496—dc22

                                                                2006032038

This book is available in quantity at special discounts for your group or organization. For further information, contact:

Triumph Books
542 South Dearborn Street
Suite 750
Chicago, Illinois 60605
(312) 939-3330
Fax (312) 663-3557

Printed in U.S.A.
ISBN: 978-1-57243-943-6
Design by Patricia Frey
All photos courtesy of AP/Wide World Photos except where otherwise indicated

To Mom, Dad, and Elizabeth.
My angels, you are always in my prayers.

Contents

Foreword

Ross Newhan has covered the Angels since 1961 for the Long Beach Press-Telegram *and the* Los Angeles Times. *He has twice served as chairman of the L.A./Anaheim chapter of the Baseball Writers' Association of America. Newhan is also the author of* The Anaheim Angels: A Complete History.

For anyone old enough to have followed the Angels since their American League inception in 1961, and to have doggedly followed them through so many seasons of inconsistent philosophy and performance, trying to envision their success in the new millennium might have been impossible. But emerging from the ashes of a history that produced more pathos than payoff, the Angels have become one of baseball's highest profile and payroll teams, one of the most consistently successful on and off the field, a perennial contender, now. They won division titles under owner Arte Moreno in 2004 and 2005 after winning their first World Series crown in 2002 under ownership of the Walt Disney Company, and the team now posts franchise attendance records almost every season—a sea of red at Angel Stadium replacing years of apathy.

Yet, while the buzz and expectation that accompanies each season now shakes the decibel meter, it is not as if the previous 40 years were played in a vacuum. Even the most casual fan, the latest to jump on the bandwagon, has a certain familiarity with the trials and torments, the highs and lows, much of it rewritten frequently in the context of the recent renaissance.

The point is that the Angels have always managed to inspire a degree of hope and an array of headlines, not all of the headlines being favorable and not all of the hope reaching fruition.

Amid strange injuries and tragic deaths, it was as if there was an Angels Curse—more self-inflicted, perhaps, than the design of a mysterious source.

Amid the consistent and failed bid to get owner Gene Autry to a World Series before he died, the "win one for the cowboy" philosophy disrupted clubhouse and front-office continuity.

There were characters—Bo Belinsky and Dean Chance set a certain tone right from the start—but not always character.

There were All-Star players—from Jim Fregosi and Buck Rodgers to Nolan Ryan and Frank Tanana, to Rod Carew and Reggie Jackson, to Dave Winfield and others—but turnover too often cut into stability.

Now, in a new century under a new owner, the Angels seem to have it together unlike ever before, and all of it, all 45 years, is fodder here for a talented writer who also knows how to put it together.

—Ross Newhan

Acknowledgments

Thanks to Tom Bast, Jess Paumier, Amy Reagan, Kelley White, Linc Wonham, and all the great folks at Triumph Books and Random House Publishing for having faith in me. Thanks also to my agent, Craig Wiley. I want to thank the Angels, a class organization all the way. Thank you to Larry Babcock and Rex Hudler.

Thanks to Karen Peterson for website support. Thank you to Bud Furillo, Ross Newhan, Robert Goldman, and Joe Haakenson. Thanks to the Baseball Hall of Fame. Thanks also to www.halosheaven.com.

Of course, my thanks as always go out to my daughter, Elizabeth Travers; my parents, Don and Inge Travers; and to my Lord and savior, Jesus Christ, who has shed his grace on thee, and to whom all glory is due!

Introduction

Elvis Would Have Played for the Angels

I am a baseball fanatic. I have been ever since I was a little kid. The Angels have *always* been a major part of my fanaticism. The team and its colorful past have had a profound impact on me, not just from a fan's standpoint, but they are intertwined in my life and development as a writer, too.

Let's start with a winter night in the 1960s. My family owned a cabin in Squaw Valley, California, site of the 1960 Olympics. We used to drive up there for ski vacations. One night my mom and dad went out to dinner, leaving me home with the babysitter, a neighbor girl. Curious, I started looking around the cabin for something with which to amuse myself. I came across a paperback book called the *1963 Official Baseball Almanac*, published by Gold Medal Books, edited by Bill Wise.

Now, this says something about me—what I'm not sure—either that I was an exception for a little kid, or that I was an exceptionally dorky little kid. Take your pick. The truth of the matter is that book was to me then like the Holy Grail. It was like the Dead Sea Scrolls. It might as well have been written in stone.

I *devoured* that book. I read every single page, absorbed every photo, memorized every statistic, mastered every nuance. It was a complete history of the 1962 Major League Baseball season. The year 1962 was a special, unique year in history. It was the year of the Cuban Missile Crisis, the last season of innocence before Dealey Plaza and Vietnam. The culture of 1962—like that of 1927—resonates in a Technicolor rainbow of nostalgia, as embodied by George Lucas's *American Graffiti*. I was too young to *remember* 1962, but the *1963*

Official Baseball Almanac turned me into a '62er of the first order. I knew *everything* about the 1962 baseball season, which was one of the greatest years in our national pastime's long history.

I took a marker and felt pens, colorizing the black-and-white photos; Dodger blue, Giant orange, Yankee pinstripes. I read every synopsis of every team, committing to memory the doings of the Twins' Camilo Pascual, the Indians' Dick Donovan, the Dodgers' Don Drysdale, the Dodgers-Giants playoff, the Mets' 120 losses, the Yankees' win in a rain-delayed, seven-game Series—all detailed in a jaunty writing style reminiscent of Walter Winchell.

But what really caught my eye was the story captivating baseball fans in the summer of '62—the Cinderella performance of a second-year expansion team, the Los Angeles Angels.

I read that book over and over again for years, well into the period in which the team became the *California* Angels. I loved that "L.A." logo. The players on the '62 team just jumped out at me. They played at Dodger Stadium. The section on the Angels started out with general manager Fred Haney quoting a poem from Sir Alfred Lord Tennyson: "'Tis better to have loved and lost than never to have loved at all," in reference to the team's flirtation with first place on Independence Day, before giving way to the Yankees. I still quote that line from Tennyson.

The guys were so darn *cocky*. Pitcher Bo Belinsky threw a no-hitter and looked to be a 20-game winner early but trailed off at the end.

"I had to do pretty good to wind up with 10–11," the self-taught playboy lefty from Jersey said. "What more do they want?"

There was a photo of Bo with manager Bill Rigney. The team story made only veiled reference to Belinsky's night-owl proclivities, but I must have picked up on something. Rigney had an exasperated, "I can't control this guy" look on his face. I drew little horns and a moustache on Belinsky to give him even more of the "handsome devil" look. This was long before I knew Mamie Van Doren from Mamie Eisenhower.

Leon "Daddy Wags" Wagner was quoted as saying that Roger Maris was "not better than me—he just makes more money."

Dean Chance disparagingly referred to Maris and Mickey Mantle as "Roger Mustard and Mickey Mayonnaise." Neither one of them could *touch* Chance. Mantle once said he got physically ill when he saw Chance's name on the lineup card!

If Elvis Presley had been a baseball player, he would have played for the 1962 Angels.

That book planted a seed that did not just turn me into a baseball fan, but a baseball *fanatic*, a historian, a chronicler. In the early 1970s, Pat Jordan wrote *The Suitors of Spring*. One of the chapters was about Belinsky (he also covered Chance). The book was excerpted in *Sports Illustrated* and remains some of the finest baseball writing ever committed to paper. The Belinsky piece may have been the greatest single article in the history of *SI*!

Maury Allen also wrote *Bo: Pitching and Wooing*, the quintessential bio of Belinsky, which I rate with *Ball Four*, *North Dallas Forty*, and *Semi-Tough* as seminal works, taking sportswriting from "hits, runs, and errors" into "sex, drugs, and rock 'n' roll"—for better or worse. I read Allen's book over and over again. It was pure fantasy. Who *was* this guy...Bo Belinsky?

In between childhood and responsibility, I was an all-conference college pitcher. One day we ventured to San Jose Municipal Stadium for a game against the San Jose State Spartans. I started and won. The southpaw pitcher on the losing end that day? Mark Langston.

I played minor league ball for the Cardinals and the A's. After having read and reread *Ball Four* and *A False Spring* numerous times, I knew exactly what to expect of minor league life. By and large, it was what I expected it to be. One night in Tennessee I struck out Kevin Mitchell three times. I was a teammate of Jose Canseco's in Idaho Falls.

I may have beaten Mr. Langston, but he did a little better at the next level. My stay was short, and I was out of baseball after a couple of years.

Fast forward to 1994. I was all grown up by then—an ex–pro baseball player, a graduate of USC and law school, an army veteran, married, divorced, and a father. *Real life.*

I had formed a sports agency with a friend and business partner. We represented Al Martin of the Pittsburgh Pirates. It turned out to be *Jerry Maguire* without the happy ending, except that in the end God steered me on my path, using a "fallen Angel" named Bo Belinsky.

One day my partner and I were sitting in the office. I had a copy of *Sports Illustrated*, which featured a classic reprint of Pat Jordan's long Belinsky excerpt, "Once He Was an Angel." I started talking about the legend that was Bo.

"Prepare to be impressed," said my partner, who was as cocky as they came. He picked up the phone and dialed a number.

"Bo Belinsky, please."

I just stared at him.

"Bo, Dave."

First-name basis.

"Great. How you doin'?"

Chitchat about some girl they knew. A date set to play golf in Las Vegas. Then...

"Bo, I got somebody who wants to speak with you," followed by the phone handed to me.

"Hello," I said.

"Hey, this is Bo. Who's this?"

The voice of Bo Belinsky. The same voice that had wooed Mamie Van Doren, Tina Louise, Ann-Margret, and Jo Collins. To make a long story short, Bo said, "Hollywood wants to make a movie about my life." He started throwing names of producers at me. Big names. A light went on in my head.

The first thing that happened after that phone call was our agency started representing Belinsky. He was still in demand at card shows and old-timers' autograph signings. We never made any money off of him, probably never even charged a commission, but hey, this was *Bo Belinsky.*

The second thing that happened was I announced that I was going to write a screenplay about Belinsky's life. Everybody looked at me like I was nuts. I had never written a screenplay in my life, although when I was majoring in communications at USC I had also taken several classes in their film school. Once upon a time, I had entertained the thought of writing—movies, sports, maybe broadcasting. When I got married, bought a house, and started a family, *real life* interfered with my plans. Instead of starting a no-pay writing career, I went to work for a stock brokerage firm, first in San Francisco, then in downtown L.A. Then I went to law school at night, went to work in the legal profession, and extended that into sports representation.

Which was where I was when I bought a paperback book about how to write screenplays at Borders. On nights and weekends I wrote the story of Belinsky's life. I contacted Maury Allen and Pat Jordan (Allen was helpful, Jordan less so), got to know Belinsky very well, and received help from "Rig" (Bill Rigney).

I entered that screenplay into one of those script contests and darned if it did not place in the quarterfinals. I started getting interest from production companies and sent copies to Oliver Stone, Robert DeNiro, and Creative Artists Agency. Eventually it was optioned by a producing team that included Frank Capra Jr. and Frank Capra III, son and grandson of the famed *It's a Wonderful Life* director. It entered into what is called in Hollywood "development hell." To date it has never been made into a movie.

The sports agency? As I say, it was *Jerry Maguire* without the happy ending. That business partner turned out to be...well, let me just say, "forgive me my trespasses, as I forgive those who trespass against me." But my Bo Belinsky screenplay turned me into a full-time professional writer. I found my passion.

I dropped out of the law and the babysitting of man-child pro athletes. I wrote 15 screenplays. My Belinsky script led to paid work, more scripts, "script doctoring," writer-for-hire assignments—the usual story. One of the scripts eventually became a movie, *The Lost Battalion*, but I was no great success in Hollywood.

I started covering high school sports for the *Los Angeles Daily News*. I also wrote for the *Los Angeles Times*. Then I landed a great gig as the star columnist for *StreetZebra*, a cool sports magazine in Marina Del Rey, but it went out of business. I was then noticed by the *San Francisco Examiner,* and I moved to the Bay Area to become their lead sports columnist. Then Barry Bonds broke the single-season home-run record. I was like the guy tagging along with Douglas MacArthur during World War II—an eyewitness to history.

The *Examiner*, for all practical purposes, went out of business, too, but God guided me through a thicket of personal and professional crises. I wrote the biography *Barry Bonds: Baseball's Superman*. It was nominated for a Casey Award for Best Baseball Book of 2002 and became a best seller.

Then I wrote 11 more books, including this one. *September 1970: One Night, Two Teams, and the Game That Changed a Nation* was the subject of a documentary on College Sports Television ("Tackling Segregation") and a major motion picture. I have written eight books for Triumph Books and Random House.

A successful writing career forged all because of Bo Belinsky. Bo passed away a few years ago, God bless him. He truly was my angel, and not a fallen one, either.

The Golden West

The 1960s: a decade that would define California, for good and ill. A decade of smog, traffic, and population growth. The greatest decade in Hollywood's history. A decade in which the sports landscape was dominated by California teams—the Dodgers, the Giants, the Lakers, the USC Trojans, and the UCLA Bruins. Ten years of monumental change. There are few decades in history that look more different at the end than they did at the beginning than the 1960s. It all started with the promise of JFK, a call to "bear any burden," to shoot for the stars. It would end with war raging in Vietnam, violence on the streets of Berkeley, drugs, and "free love" in Golden Gate Park.

In November of 1960, John F. Kennedy defeated Vice President Richard M. Nixon to become president of the United States. There was evidence that the election had been stolen via multiple votes in Cook County, Illinois ("vote early, vote often") and "tombstone ballots" in Texas. The Republican standard bearer, Nixon, decided not to challenge the closest election in U.S. history.

Before the senate and then the vice presidency, Nixon had been a congressman representing a district that stretched from parts of Orange County into Los Angeles. The man who would sit astride the decade to come began it in defeat, returning to his hometown. He bought a home in Beverly Hills, taking a job with a corporate law firm in downtown L.A. At around this same time, Nixon was approached by an ownership group, led by the Los Angeles Dodgers' Walter O'Malley. Would he like to be the next commissioner of baseball?

Nixon was an enormous baseball fan who, when he got the call in 1955 that President Dwight Eisenhower had suffered a heart

IF ONLY . . . Charlie O. Finley had succeeded in acquiring ownership of L.A.'s expansion franchise instead of Gene Autry, he may well have left town when attendance suffered in the 1960s (instead of moving to Orange County), and there might not have been Major League Baseball in Oakland. Or, on the flip side, he might have built a dynasty like he did in Oakland, overshadowing the Dodgers.

attack, meaning he was now a "heartbeat away from the presidency," was poring over the Sunday baseball statistics in the *Washington Post*.

Baseball wanted a Californian. The Los Angeles Dodgers and San Francisco Giants had made the move to the coast. The sensibilities and trends of a nation were looking to the West.

Nixon still had political ambitions. Aside from his legal work, he was committed to writing *Six Crises*, and next up would be a run for governor of California, which was supposed to set him up for another White House campaign in 1964 or 1968. He turned down the ownership group, which set up some interesting "if only" scenarios.

The Dodgers and Giants were not the only new California franchises. The Los Angeles Chargers and Oakland Raiders were members of the fledgling American Football League. The Minneapolis Lakers of the NBA were now the L.A. Lakers.

The immediate success of the Dodgers and Giants, which fueled the building of Dodger Stadium and Candlestick Park, created the impetus for expansion. In the National League, New York and Houston. In the American League, another team in L.A., as well as Minneapolis–St. Paul.

A millionaire, midwestern insurance salesman named Charlie O. Finley set his sights on the Los Angeles franchise. He had the money and certainly the ambition, but he lacked...imprimatur.

One man did not lack imprimatur, or *gravitas*, or star power; pick the cliché, but Gene Autry, "the Singing Cowboy," was a household name, a Hollywood superstar, and an American icon.

As a businessman, everything Autry touched turned to gold. One of those enterprises was the Golden West Radio Network, which consisted of several stations in California. Freeway construction, a commuter culture, suburban growth, and sports programming meant that it was a new "golden age" for radio and boom times for Golden West.

Autry's ownership of Golden West meant two things: he was awarded the ownership of the Angels franchise, and he became a rival of Walter O'Malley. O'Malley was not pleased that his territory would have to be shared, especially since he was taking on the economic burdens of building Dodger Stadium. The Dodgers' radio station was KMPC, part of Autry's Golden West network. But O'Malley had a vacation home in the mountains, at Lake Arrowhead. When he went there for a visit, he was disturbed that the Dodgers signal did not reach his resort. O'Malley broke from KMPC, switching to the high-wattage KFI.

"I was shocked," Autry was quoted as saying in Ross Newhan's *The Anaheim Angels: A Complete History.* "Bob Reynolds, my partner,

Gene Autry, "the Singing Cowboy," was a household name, a Hollywood superstar, and an American icon. As a businessman, virtually everything Autry touched turned to gold.

TOP 10

All-Time Greatest Sports Owners

	Owner	Team
1.	Art Rooney	Pittsburgh Steelers
2.	Connie Mack	Philadelphia A's
3.	Walter O'Malley	Los Angeles Dodgers
4.	Bill Veeck	Cleveland Indians, Chicago White Sox
5.	Gene Autry	California Angels
6.	Wellington Mara	New York Giants
7.	George Halas	Chicago Bears
8.	Philip K. Wrigley	Chicago Cubs
9.	August A. Busch	St. Louis Cardinals
10.	Lamar Hunt	Kansas City Chiefs

and Stan Spero, my general manager at KMPC, had personally negotiated with O'Malley and believed they had his word on contract renewal."

Autry's station had played an instrumental role in the public promotion of Dodger Stadium's erection. Miffed, he decided that instead of being one of O'Malley's partners—a role that everybody from Branch Rickey to jilted New York politicos already knew was fraught with peril—he would become his competitor.

Autry initially became involved in the process of acquiring the new L.A. team's radio contract. Bill Veeck was the point man in the new ownership group. O'Malley *did not* want to share Los Angeles with a man of Veeck's considerable marketing skills. He demanded a $450,000 "territorial rights" fee.

A "war," similar to the ongoing battles between the AFL and NFL, threatened to break out in baseball. Veeck was out. Finley entered the picture, as did Yankees co-owner and hotel magnate Del Webb. Webb was a friend and associate of Autry's. Discussions were entered into, with Autry seen by all as a suitable owner, along with partner Bob Reynolds, a former Stanford football star.

Autry and Reynolds co-owned KMPC, bidding for the Angels with the broadcast rights of the station providing an enticement.

KMPC had once carried Hollywood Stars games. American League president Joe Cronin had known Autry a long time. A "letter of credit" for $1.5 million was drawn up. Former Milwaukee Braves general manager Fred Haney was brought into the group. To satisfy O'Malley and the National League, it was agreed that the senior circuit would expand into the South and back into the biggest market, New York.

Autry and Reynolds were approved on December 7, 1960, a date that will live in infamy, but final approval had to come from O'Malley.

Autry and O'Malley met in O'Malley's suite at the Park Plaza Hotel in St. Louis, lasting until 3:00 in the morning. O'Malley forced Autry into a bad financial arrangement in which the Angels would rent Dodger Stadium for four years, pay $2.1 million for players in the "expansion draft," and pay $350,000 for L.A.'s "grazing rights."

Autry told Reynolds that he would not be happy with the arrangement, but they all knew that dealing with O'Malley was warfare. They were just happy to have survived and looked forward to owning a baseball team in 1961.

Haney, one of the most respected baseball men in the game, was immediately hired as the team's general manager. The next choice would be the club's field manager. There were three obvious candidates.

Leo Durocher, the former manager of the Brooklyn Dodgers and New York Giants, was famous and controversial. He lived in Beverly Hills and cultivated Hollywood friendships. He was also "black-balled" by baseball, having offended most everybody of importance. Through writer Mel Durslag, Durocher had written a public "explanation to my friends" in 1960, in which he stated that it was not his choice to be out of baseball and he wanted back in. But Haney wanted nothing to do with brash Durocher. The Dodgers immediately hired him as a "celebrity coach," causing enormous headaches for manager Walter Alston.

The next choice was Casey Stengel, recently fired as manager of the Yankees. Stengel lived in Glendale and seemed perfect. However, he had signed a lucrative deal to write his memoirs for the *Saturday Evening Post*, requiring he stay out of baseball until its publication.

DID YOU KNOW . . . That the man who first informed America of the creation of the Angels, to be owned by Gene Autry and Bob Reynolds, was a young L.A. reporter working for the Golden West Radio Network named Lon Simmons? The network also included KSFO in San Francisco. Through that connection, Simmons joined the Giants' broadcast team of Russ Hodges and Bill King. Today, Simmons is in the Broadcaster's Wing of the National Baseball Hall of Fame.

He also had taken the job as vice president of a Glendale bank and needed to spend some time in that capacity. He would go on to manage the New York Mets a year later.

That left Bill Rigney, a one-time New York Giants journeyman who had managed Willie Mays when the club moved to San Francisco but had been fired after failing to nail down the pennant in close races. He had no baggage, was eager for the job, and was hired.

Wrigley Field

The Pacific Coast League was, for all practical purposes, the *major* leagues before the Dodgers and big-league Angels took up residence on the West Coast. After World War I, the best athletes in the world consistently came from California. The Golden State produced more star big leaguers than any other state. Most of them played in the PCL before ascending to the majors.

The San Francisco Seals had featured the likes of Joe DiMaggio, Tony Lazzeri, Paul Waner, Lloyd Waner, and Lefty O'Doul. Casey Stengel, whose star second baseman was Billy Martin, managed the Oakland Oaks. The San Diego Padres once had a teenage pitcher named Ted Williams.

Two teams played in Los Angeles. The Hollywood Stars played their games where the current CBS-TV center is. The Los Angeles Angels played at Wrigley Field. With a tall Spanish-style clocktower, Wrigley Field was a landmark that could be seen from miles around in South Central Los Angeles.

Wrigley Field was named after its owner, Philip K. Wrigley, the same owner and namesake of Chicago's Wrigley Field. Wrigley completely dropped the ball when it came to the West Coast baseball vision. It was his and he let it get away.

Wrigley's Chicago Cubs trained at Catalina Island, off the L.A. coast. According to legend, Cubs broadcaster Ronald Reagan was in town for spring training. As a lark, he arranged for a studio screen test. This led to his acting career. The Cubs team in the PCL played at Wrigley. Had Wrigley wanted to control the big-league expansion to California, he could have done so. Instead he sat idly by while

Walter O'Malley rode the whirlwind, which helps explain why the Cubs were always mediocre, the Dodgers always excellent.

O'Malley purchased Wrigley Field from Wrigley. This meant that he had the stadium and the name "Angels" as bargaining chips on that December night with Autry, both of which Autry had to pay extra for. But O'Malley had eschewed Wrigley Field as a temporary home for his Dodgers. Instead of the 22,000-seat stadium, he arranged to play at the 92,000-seat L.A. Coliseum, despite it being built for football.

While it appeared that O'Malley had all the chips, Autry scored a major coup when he arranged for the Angels to train in Palm Springs.

An aerial view of Wrigley Field, where the Los Angeles Angels played their first game on April 27, 1961. The stadium was demolished in 1966.

The Dodgers were committed to Vero Beach, Florida. Dodgertown was baseball's finest spring-training facility, and O'Malley wanted to maintain the East Coast fan base from Brooklyn.

TRIVIA

Which teams made up the core of the Pacific Coast League before big-league ball came to the West Coast?

Answers to the trivia questions are on pages 189–190.

Baseball teams had started to train in Arizona after World War II, and of course the Cubs had trained in Catalina, but that was so far off the beaten path, it was problematic. Palm Springs was perfect for the Angels. It was only a two-hour drive from L.A. but accessible to and from the Arizona spring camps. More importantly, Palm Springs and Autry gave the Angels Hollywood flair.

Along with Las Vegas, it was by 1961 a popular resort destination, favored by the show biz crowd. Bob Hope, Dean Martin, and Frank Sinatra were just a few of the celebrities who played its golf courses. Ex-President Dwight Eisenhower loved to tee it up there. Rigney invited him into the dugout and had him "manage" for an inning. Ike protested, but Rig assured him that if he could win the war and plan D-day, running his club was not a problem.

Pretty girls lounged by the Palm Springs swimming pools in the 100-degree heat. For an old song-and-dance icon like Gene Autry, it was an ideal place to showcase his team. He wanted the Angels to reflect all the Tinsel Town glitz that they could.

When the equipment manager opened the box containing the team's first uniforms, the stylized *L.A.* logo and the halo on the cap impressed everybody. Haney and Rigney did a masterful job drafting and building a roster. There was a perfect blend of youth and veterans. Established players like pitcher Eli Grba, first basemen Ted Kluszewski and Lee Thomas, and minor league icon Steve Bilko, gave the team early name recognition. Younger players like Albie Pearson, Dean Chance, Ken McBride, Jim Fregosi, and Buck Rodgers were purchased and would pay dividends soon enough.

Bilko was a local superstar who had put up enormous PCL power numbers in the 1950s. He was an immediate crowd favorite. The first game at Wrigley Field featured Tony Martin singing the

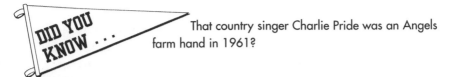

That country singer Charlie Pride was an Angels farm hand in 1961?

national anthem. Then, 11, 931 fans saw Ty Cobb, a California resident, throw out the first ball in the last month of his life.

The 1961 Angels won 70 games, a remarkable feat considering their expansion status. The other first-year team, the Washington Senators (who replaced the original Senators, now the Minnesota Twins) was woeful. The following year the expansion Mets, trying to duplicate the Angels formula of veterans but without any youthful supporting cast, lost 120 games.

Outfielder Leon Wagner, considered expendable by both the San Francisco Giants and the St. Louis Cardinals, came over and immediately provided power. Along with Ken Hunt and Albie Pearson, a defensive wizard who could get on base and provided speed on the base paths, the Angels had a creditable outfield.

Tom Satriano from USC came up toward the end of 1961, as did Jim Fregosi and Dean Chance. Bilko slammed 20 home runs.

Veteran pitchers Tom Morgan and Art Fowler were effective. Ryne Duren still threw pellets. A great talent, Duren had come up as a relief pitcher with the Yankees. He wore glasses described as "Coke bottles." His first warm-up pitch was usually a 100-mph fastball into the screen beyond the batter's box, a testament to his wildness and willingness to send a "message" to the frightened hitter waiting on deck.

Duren might have been a Hall of Famer had he controlled his pitches or his drinking, but alas, neither would be tamed during his career. But he was a favorite of Rigney's and the fans' in 1961. After retirement, no longer enticed by the road, he found sobriety.

Many people have said that it was expansion and cozy Wrigley Field that caused Roger Maris to break Babe Ruth's record with 61 home runs in 1961. The truth is that, while a big-league-record 248 homers were hit at Wrigley (with Bilko, Wagner, Hunt, Thomas, and Earl Averill all hitting more than 20), Maris and Mickey Mantle only hit a total of four between them.

The Angels had several ex-Yankees who apparently knew how to pitch to the Yankees sluggers. Over the next years, Mantle would have little success in L.A. for two reasons: he partied heavily whenever in town, and he could not touch Dean Chance.

The Angels drew 603,510 fans in their first year. Considering everything, it was considered a success. Hopes were high for the future. The Dodgers, of course, drew well at the Coliseum, where Sandy Koufax was finally coming into his own, and the club finished second to Cincinnati.

The last game played at Wrigley Field was on October 1, 1961. The stadium stood for five more years, falling to the wrecking crew in 1966. It is a distant, nostalgic memory in the life of L.A. sporting annals.

Bill Rigney in the City of Angels

When this author pitched in the Oakland organization, I had a chance to get to know Bill Rigney personally. In 1994 I wrote a screenplay, *Once He Was an Angel,* about former southpaw Bo Belinsky, who pitched for Rig. Even though I had not been a major prospect with the A's, Rig remembered me and gave me valuable insight into that period. One funny anecdote involved a friend of mine, Kevin McCormack, who for years would call my house and identify himself to my dad as some well-known sports figure; say, Reggie Jackson or Vin Scully. One day Rig called me. My dad answered, asked who was on the line, and Rig said, "Bill Rigney." My dad said, "Yeah, right, Mac," before recognizing the voice as Rig's.

In writing the screenplay—I had always had a fascination with the era—I became an expert on a state of mind called "Hollywood" during that golden time, circa 1962. Rig, who also spent years in New York, would be the first to tell you that his L.A. experience was probably the most colorful of his long career.

There are some years that stand out, encapsulating a certain time; 1962 is one of those years. George Lucas's *American Graffiti* was set in '62, when an innocent country had not yet gone to Vietnam, John Glenn circled the Earth, and missiles in Cuba had schoolchildren practicing the Cold War drill of ducking under desks.

It was a particularly good California sports season, too. The undefeated Trojans of Southern Cal ushered in the John McKay era with a national championship. The National League pennant race was a bitter, down-to-the-playoffs death match between new West Coast rivals, the Dodgers and Giants.

DID YOU KNOW . . . That the early 1960s were not just a golden age of baseball in Los Angeles, but the beginning of the Golden Age in Hollywood? Great films of the era included Spartacus (1960); One, Two, Three (1961); The Manchurian Candidate (1962); Lawrence of Arabia (1962), Seven Days in May (1963); Dr. Strangelove (1964); and Cool Hand Luke (1967).

But 1962 was not supposed to be a memorable year for the Los Angeles Angels. An expansion team in 1961, the Angels were a creditable 70–91 in their first year, playing at dilapidated Wrigley Field in South Central L.A., at the corner of 42nd Place and Avalon Boulevard. In '62 they rented Dodger Stadium from Walter O'Malley. The Dodgers were the toast of Hollywood. The Angels, a combination of cast-offs and kids, were tenants who played before family and friends. The first Angel to receive attention was southpaw pitcher Bo Belinsky. The Angels thought he would attract female fans (he did). Another rookie, Dean Chance, was an emerging star, winning 14 games. Former Giant Leon "Daddy Wags" Wagner hit 37 home runs and knocked in 107 runs.

Belinsky started the year living in Ernie's House of Surface with Lakers wildman "Hot Rod" Hundley, but apparently Bo's consumption of women and alcohol was too much even for the Rodster. Belinsky then moved his act to the Hollywood Hills, where some adoring girl almost killed herself trying to climb a tree into his bedroom window. When Belinsky was not wining and dining Tina Louise, Mamie Van Doren, and Ann-Margret, he was winning games. By August, an early-morning run-in with the LAPD and escapades with the Hollywood crowd had slowed his win total down, but the man had put the club on the map.

On July 4, Los Angeles was in first place in the American League. Bill Rigney and Fred Haney were shrewd baseball men. Rig had been schooled under Leo Durocher in New York. Haney had developed the great Milwaukee Braves' pennant winners of 1957–1958. The Yankees, led by Mickey Mantle and Roger Maris, were at the height of their dynasty that year.

The Angels played them tough, finally succumbing in the dog days of late August and September. Their 86–76 record earned

Bill Rigney (right), shown with player Albie Pearson in 1962, thoroughly enjoyed and embraced the halcyon days of 1960s Southern California.
Photo courtesy of Getty Images.

14

Rigney Manager of the Year honors. Haney was named Executive of the Year. Chance was the best rookie pitcher in the game. Movie stars like Cary Grant and Doris Day cheered them on.

"Chance was the best pitcher I ever managed," Rigney said of the 1964 Cy Young Award winner, back when he was advising me on *Once He Was an Angel.* "He was a farmboy who started hanging out with Bo and the Hollywood crowd. Oh, what a pistol those two were! But he was the best chucker from the right I ever saw," which was an amazing statement.

What about Belinsky?

"Oh, my," said Rigney, who had a shock of white hair. "He's the reason I had white hair." Behind his back, Belinsky called him "the White Rat."

"He also looked like a cab driving down the street with the doors open," recalled Belinsky of Rigney's rather oversized ears.

Rigney and Belinsky feuded from 1962 to 1964, when Bo was arrested for throwing a lovesick showgirl out of his "lipstick red" Cadillac, later assaulted *L.A. Times* sportswriter Braven Dyer, and showed up "reeking

TRIVIA

Who was Bob Case?

Answers to the trivia questions are on pages 189–190.

of booze and broads," only to find the club's Boston hotel burning down.

"See me at the ballpark first thing in the morning," was all Rigney said to Belinsky. Rig had thought Bo was burning up inside when he observed him trying to "blend in" with the pajama-wearing group.

"Rig was always trying to hit on Mamie when I'd bring her to team parties," recalled Belinsky, who lived in Las Vegas until his 2001 passing. "They all tried to get in her pants. Every time I'd get in trouble, Rig would call me on the carpet and say he was my friend, but behind my back he'd say I was bad for the game."

Rigney certainly had no hard feelings. He said his sole motivation in helping the research of a screenplay about Belinsky's life was, "I'll do it if it helps Bo."

An older, mellower Belinsky had fond memories of his old manager.

"If I'd listened to him then," he said in 1994, "I would have had a much better career."

Belinsky was unable to control his taste for wine, women, and song. Some of the others proved to be one-year wonders. The team moved to Anaheim. By the time they fired Rigney in 1969, their Sunset Strip personality was gone. Some say an "Angels Curse" has hung over them in the form of various tragedies and quirks of fate that have befallen players wearing the halo. The nostalgic memory of the Sunset Strip "Summer of '62," however, remained, in many ways, the highlight of their history until the 2002 World Championship season.

"Working for Gene Autry, managing Bo Belinsky, and dealing with Hollywood," Rig said of the 1962 season, "made that the most interesting year of my career."

Once He Was an Angel

"Once He Was an Angel" was the name of Pat Jordan's chapter—excerpted in *Sports Illustrated*—about Bo Belinsky in his masterful book, *The Suitors of Spring*. It was one of the names of this author's screenplay based on Maury Allen's book, *Bo: Pitching and Wooing*. Other life forms included *Fallen Angel,* among other things.

For several years, Bo and I went through the odyssey of trying to get that script made into a movie. Getting to know Bo Belinsky personally turned out to be one of the most fascinating experiences of my life. I revisited the Belinsky epic in 1999 when, as a columnist for the L.A. sports magazine *StreetZebra*, I wrote a "Distant Replay" about him.

The story of Belinsky and the Angels in those early years is so interesting because the team's character was utterly different from what modern fans came to know about the team in Anaheim. It was night and day. In 1962 they rented Chavez Ravine and were owned by "the Singing Cowboy," Gene Autry, who was old Hollywood all the way. Autry thought that cocksure rookie southpaw Belinsky might just sell tickets. Belinsky had garnered his "15 minutes of fame" holding out for the enormous sum of $6,500. Writer Bud Furillo captured some of Bo's choice comments about women, sex, and hustling pool on a slow news day.

Fred Haney tired of negotiating with Belinksy over the phone. He sensed that if he were brought out to Palm Springs, it would create needed publicity in the shadow of the mighty Dodgers. He was right.

"He was the greatest thing to ever happen to us," said publicity director Irv Kaze, who enthusiastically supported our movie efforts in his later role of sports talk show host. Kaze showed up at the

DID YOU KNOW . . . That one of Bo Belinsky's favorite Sunset Strip haunts was the famed Whisky A Go Go? The Whisky gave rise to such 1960s L.A. acts as The Doors, The Byrds, Jan and Dean, and The Jefferson Airplane, among many others. Belinsky once played pool with Jim Morrison of The Doors and rubbed elbows with numerous superstars, usually before they were famous.

airport and, without having to ask, immediately recognized Belinsky, oozing charisma in an open-collared shirt, sportcoat, long slick hair, and "the biggest pair of sunglasses you've ever seen."

"Damn," said Belinsky when Kaze introduced himself, "I expected Autry."

Bo was immediately driven to the Palm Springs Desert Inn, where Kaze arranged for a poolside press conference complete with a full bar and strategically placed bikini-clad girls lounging about. For a couple of hours, Belinsky regaled them with stories of his pool-hustling exploits, which made him out to sound like "Minnesota Fats."

His sexual descriptions were explicit. Nobody had ever heard anything like this guy, and in all probability nobody has ever heard anything like him since. As a "kiss and tell" artist, Belinsky put Jose Canseco, Derek Jeter, and even Joe Namath to shame. The bizarre poolside scene—part carnival act, part "true confessions," part striptease show—was "the greatest thing I'd ever seen," recalled Kaze. All of this cost between $1,000–$1,500 in 1962 for an unproven career minor leaguer who said he would not sign "unless Autry begged [him] personally."

For three days, Belinsky never suited up or came close to "training" for baseball, preferring instead to seek out those bikini-clad "chickies" by day and night. Finally, Haney called him and said, "This is enough." A gentlemen's agreement to renegotiate if Belinsky made the club and proved himself was hammered out.

Thus did Bo have his motivation. Out of shape, and continually distracted by the Palm Springs "scenery," he inspired nobody on the mound, however. Rigney wanted to ship him out. Haney tried to trade him back to the Baltimore organization, where he had been before getting plucked in the minor league draft. They had seen all of Belinsky's act they could handle.

While in the Orioles chain, he had to be snuck out of one town when an underage girl whose mother was seeing the chief of detectives, threatened to cry rape if he did not marry her.

Earl Weaver watched in despair when Belinsky and Joe Pepitone would somehow find hot nightspots in Aberdeen, South Dakota. In Miami Bo hooked up with a married woman. Later he found himself drinking with her husband, an army general, and in a moment of supreme honesty he owned up to being the guy she had left with, offering a toast with the statement, "We sure had a helluva time with your money." He had gone AWOL in Mexico. Orioles pitchers Steve Dalkowski, Steve Barber, and Belinsky were fined by Baltimore manager Paul Richards for drilling holes in Bo's hotel room to sneak a peak at the reigning Miss Universe staying next door.

Like Rod Steiger rejecting Sidney Poitier's offer of "pity" in *In the Heat of the Night*, the Orioles said, "No, thank you," to Haney.

Autry stepped in and, in a rare act of ownership control, informed his employees that Belinsky was to make the squad, at

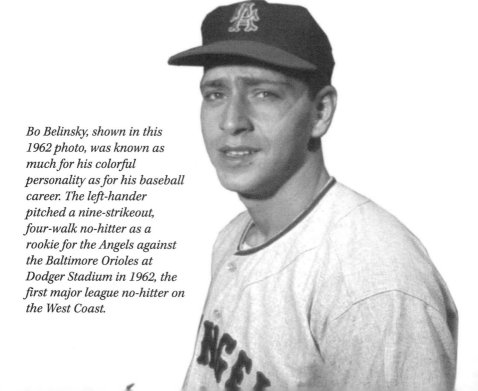

Bo Belinsky, shown in this 1962 photo, was known as much for his colorful personality as for his baseball career. The left-hander pitched a nine-strikeout, four-walk no-hitter as a rookie for the Angels against the Baltimore Orioles at Dodger Stadium in 1962, the first major league no-hitter on the West Coast.

Baseball Books of All-Time

1. *Ball Four* by Jim Bouton
2. *The Summer Game* by Roger Angell
3. *The Glory of Their Times* by Lawrence Ritter
4. *The Boys of Summer* by Roger Kahn
5. *Bo: Pitching and Wooing* by Maury Allen (Angels)
6. *False Spring* by Pat Jordan
7. *October 1964* by David Halberstam
8. *The Wrong Stuff* by Bill "Spaceman" Lee
9. *Moneyball* by Michael Lewis
10. *The Suitors of Spring* by Pat Jordan (Angels)

least for the first few weeks of the regular season. His hope was that the spring-training publicity might sell a few tickets. Rig was none too pleased but carried out the order. Then injuries depleted his rotation. On April 18 Belinsky was given an emergency start against Kansas City at Dodger Stadium.

Given the news of his start the next day, Bo went out to the Sunset Strip, made "friends," and finally fell asleep around 5:00 AM.

"Sex always relaxed me; nobody ever died from it," Bo told Maury Allen in 1972.

In the locker room, Rigney handed him the game ball and said simply, "Win or be gone."

Bo won 3–2. It earned him a second start, which turned out to be a complete game victory against Cleveland. When he won in his next start the publicity was enormous and of a national character. Bud Furillo's original story had made the wire services. His Palm Springs quotes received major attention. Suddenly Bo was the subject of every media report. He was invited to major Hollywood parties. Actresses and starlets were calling him.

Then, on May 4, 1962, the Strip was hopping with Mexican festivities for Cinco de Mayo. Belinsky, scheduled to pitch the next night, made the scene, where he met a lovely brunette. They spent the evening at her pad. Belinsky departed with the dawn's early light, but this encounter inspired him. He asked for her phone number and meant it.

"I'll see you again," she assured him. Belinsky told her he was leaving tickets for that night's game against Baltimore and insisted she make it because, "You're my lucky charm."

"I never saw her again," Bo told Pat Jordan in 1972. "It was like she was my lucky charm and once she was gone, that was the end of that."

Eventually, maybe, but first Bo Belinsky was about to skyrocket to the heights of Hollywood fame and glory. That evening he threw a no-hit, no-run game against his old team.

"I did it first," he told Jordan in a drunken fit, "before Marichal or Koufax or any of those f*ckers."

Angel's Flight

The Bo Belinsky phenomenon cannot be accurately described within these pages. Some compared it to "Fernandomania." Others have seen similarities to "Broadway Joe" Namath and the "Super Jets." But nothing quite fits. Never has an athlete come out of nowhere so fast, gotten so much hype, and lived off it so highly in such a quicksilver manner.

Between 1962 and 1964 Bo Belinsky, who was talented but never lived up to his potential beyond the night of May 5, 1962, was the most publicized athlete in the nation. More than Sandy Koufax, Willie Mays, Johnny Unitas, Wilt Chamberlain, or Bill Russell—all superstars of the era.

"I don't know that there were more words written about Bo than anybody else," Maury Allen said in 1999, "but he was up there." This despite an ultimately losing record in 1962 and a bad 1963, in which he was demoted to the minors.

The immediate rewards of the no-hitter were proffered. His contract was increased to the promised $8,500, and he received a "lipstick red" Cadillac as a gift from the club. Bud Furillo assumed the role of Bo's "social director," introducing him to Beverly Hills attorney Paul Caruso, who in turn introduced him to the controversial gossip columnist and movie voice, Walter Winchell.

Winchell was the staccato voiceover of the TV show *The Untouchables*, starring Robert Stack as Eliot Ness. Winchell used his New York column to rail against communist infiltration during the McCarthy era. McCarthy's demise put Winchell on the outs in New York.

Winchell had moved to Hollywood to reinvent himself. He had a showbiz column and was looking for material. When Furillo introduced Belinsky to the showbiz crowd, the Belinsky-Winchell relationship became a marriage made in...Hollywood.

"I know every broad who matters," Winchell told Bo. Winchell arranged through his publicity contacts for every aspiring model and actress in L.A. to date Bo Belinsky, alerting the press to each liaison so that it could all be dutifully recorded in the trades.

Gilligan's Island beauty Tina Louise; actress Connie Stevens (and her younger, blonder sister); Dinah Shore; Queen Soraya, the ex-wife of the Shah of Iran; a DuPont heiress; *Carnal Knowledge* star Ann-Margret; Belinsky squired all of them and many more to every haunt

In many ways Bo Belinsky personified glamorous and glitzy Hollywood and the freewheeling 1960s during his heyday. Photo courtesy of Getty Images.

on the Sunset Strip: Peppermint West, Barney's Beanery, Dino's, Chasen's, LaScala, The Rainbow, Gazarri's, The Whisky.

He found himself invited to party with the beautiful people: Jane Wyman, Merle Oberon, Maureen O'Hara, Frank Sinatra, Lionel Hampton. In New York he was fêted by Toots Shor, given tables reserved for celebrities and mobsters at the Copa, The Forum of the Twelve Caesars, and 21.

In Washington, Belinsky and Dean Chance were told that FBI Director J. Edgar Hoover wanted to meet them.

"Jesus Christ, they're turning it into a federal case," exclaimed Chance, who thought Hoover's invite was an inquest into some kind of illegal interstate activity. Hoover just wanted to meet them.

"J. Edgar?" Belinsky later told Pat Jordan. "Man, he's a swinger. He let Dean and I shoot Tommy guns at FBI headquarters."

As the season played out, Bo continued to "pitch and woo." His record went to 6–1, but then he began to lose. Off the field, he was as wild as ever. Naturally, Rigney and Haney questioned whether he could effectively pitch on little or no rest. The papers and trades were filled with near-daily Belinsky items, mostly fed by Winchell. Madonna at her hottest never got so much attention. Belinsky courted it. He never hid from the publicity. He ate it up with a fork and spoon.

The team would arrive at L.A. International Airport in the wee hours of the morning, hoping only to get home and sleep. Bo would be met by not one but two delicious girls. He would depart into the L.A. night, leaving his bags to the equipment manager while his teammates watched in awe and wonder, exploding into an ovation.

He moved into a Hollywood Hills pad that had once been occupied by Pablo Picasso, who had painted a mural on the wall of what was now Belinsky's living room.

The club tolerated it because the publicity was good for business, the team was winning, Bo was still effective, and Autry admired his employee's style. But a 5:00 AM incident on Wilshire Boulevard brought everything to a boil. Belinsky and Chance went out for a night on the town, picking up two girls. Bo's was some kind of showgirl, or so she said. The four of them piled into Bo's "lipstick red" Caddy.

TOP 10

Greatest Sports Playboys

1. Bo Bolincky
2. Joe Namath
3. Babe Ruth
4. Mike Piazza
5. Derek Sanderson
6. Walt Frazier
7. Derek Jeter
8. Frank Tanana
9. Johnny Bench
10. Wes Parker

"Now we are tooling down Wilshire Boulevard and everything is fine," Belinsky recalled. "Well, one thing led to another, and this girl starts mouthing off about she loves me and will stay with me and wants to cook breakfast and all that bull. I'm really in no mood for that, so I tell her to keep her big mouth shut or I'll throw her out."

According to Belinsky, the girl kept yakking, so he pulled the car over to a side street, demanding that she get out. She resisted. Bo tried to force her out. In the process she smashed her head against a window, cutting herself, and causing her to start screaming bloody murder.

Just then, an LAPD squad car pulled up. Chance, who had a pregnant wife back in Ohio, made a run for it but was caught. Arrests were made, and it all hit the papers, to the great consternation of Haney and Rigney.

The girl decided not to press charges on the condition that Bo stay with her for a week, but she later found an attorney and sued Belinsky, forcing him to pay her off.

"You just can't trust broads," was Bo's assessment.

While all of this was happening, Belinsky discovered to his chagrin that the "lipstick red" Caddy, a "gift" from the club, was late in payments. He assumed that it was paid for in full. Instead, he had

IF ONLY . . . The early Angels had taken better advantage of the Southern California talent base, they might have improved faster than they did. The original decision involved a mixture of veterans and youth, which worked until the veterans got old. Southern California, and Orange County in particular, is renowned for producing great talent, yet the team did not take advantage of the pre-draft formula in which they could have signed regional stars left and right. USC was easily the best college baseball program in the nation, but only Tom Satriano came to the Angels from there.

to assume the monthly installments plus insurance payments. He was trying to live the life of Frank Sinatra on $8,500.

The Angels, in first place on July 4, pushed the Yankees into August before tailing off toward the end, but the season was a spectacular success for a second-year team. Their veterans had played well, and youth was served. The future looked bright.

Bo finished 10–11, a disappointment after starting 5–0 with a no-hitter, but a solid year nevertheless. The team's brass held its breath, hoping that perhaps he would mature, calm down, and make use of his natural talents in a way that would allow him to enjoy a good career for the Angels.

Fallen Angel

If his off-season activities were any indication, this hope looked to be more of a pipe dream. Belinsky spent the winter performing in a Vegas lounge act surrounded by young lovelies dressed in skintight baseball suits. He did screen tests for movies, which, according to every Hollywood agent and producer, were in the offing. Plans were made for him to star in a Western which he dubbed "The Last Shoot-Out at Bo's Corral."

Spring training got off to a rough start when Belinsky met up with a companion in Palm Springs. They retired to his hotel room, where they ordered a full array of room service hors d'ouvres and champagne, all *charged to the ballclub*. They then started to "go after it hammer and tongs," until somebody's feet knocked over the tray, causing bottles and dishes to fall in a crashing of broken glass.

The next day they tiptoed around the crash scene, the girl departing and Bo heading to the ballpark. A maid discovered the broken glass and informed the hotel manager, who contacted Haney.

"Don't tell me who," said Haney.

"Yes," the manager said, "it's him again."

A fine ensued; 1963 was a bad year. The team's veterans got old fast. The fast 'n' loose style of the Angels caught up with them. Belinsky was 1–7 when the team sent him to the minor leagues.

Salt Lake City? Albuquerque? Omaha?

No. Honolulu.

"It was the best place of my career," Bo said. "Hawaii's better than a lot of big-league towns. I'd have been happy to play my whole career there. It was relaxing for me, it got me out of that whole

All-1960s Angels

Position	Name
Pitcher	Dean Chance
Pitcher	Andy Messersmith
Pitcher	Ken McBride
Pitcher	Jim McGlothlin
Relief Pitcher	Minnie Rojas
Catcher	Buck Rodgers
First Baseman	Don Mincher
Second Baseman	Bobby Knoop
Third Baseman	Aurelio Rodriguez
Shortstop	Jim Fregosi
Outfielder	Leon "Daddy Wags" Wagner
Outfielder	Albie Pearson
Outfielder	Rick Reichardt
Manager	Bill Rigney

Hollywood scene. I pitched great there, and I've never seen so many beautiful girls in my life."

Belinsky did pitch well in Hawaii—well enough to earn a promotion back to Los Angeles, which of course got him right back into the limelight of publicity, Hollywood, and all those starlets.

One of those starlets was the actress Mamie Van Doren, a blonde bombshell who at the time was being groomed by the movie industry into becoming the next Marilyn Monroe and Jayne Mansfield. Stardom eluded Van Doren, but she and Belinsky became a major item. She knew he was great publicity for her career. The two became inseparable items around town, their images splashed all over the trade papers.

Eventually, Mamie told Bud Furillo that they were engaged. Furillo ensured that the headlines were the same size as "FIDEL DEAD," but it was all news to Bo. Pressured, he bought Van Doren a big rock, but they immediately began to argue, and the engagement was called off. Relieved of the pressure, the romance bloomed again, but neither one was faithful to the other, so they decided to call it quits before hurting each other further.

Belinsky wanted the ring back, but Van Doren refused, until he hired a private dick who presented evidence that she was not exactly lonely.

"Mamie's got a little class," Bo told the media. "Very little."

In 1964 Dean Chance put together one of those seasons that happens every so often. Like Ron Guidry in 1978 and Orel Hershiser in 1988, Chance caught fire and *could not be hit.* His sidekick, Belinsky, seemed to pick up his momentum. In the first four and a half months of the season it seemed that, finally, their collective potential had been reached.

Bo continued to party. His success on the field had little to do with his off-field "success." By this point he was a personality separate from his baseball persona. Every bar owner, every actress and model, every socialite wanted him to be a part of the scene, and he obliged. Somehow, he seemed in '64 to have managed a way to compartmentalize this life with the demands of a baseball career.

He was only 9–8 in August, but as his 2.87 ERA demonstrated, he pitched great ball, the victim of brutal offensive support from an Angels club that had lost all their offensive firepower from the magical summer of '62.

Thanks to Bo and Dean Chance, the team was still popular. Sandy Koufax was out for the season with an injury. Without him the Dodgers fell by the wayside, giving their junior tenants a unique chance to grab some serious market share in the City of Angels.

Looking back to that August, it seems the events which transpired that month changed the very nature of the franchise. An age came to an end, replaced by a strange twist of fate, a change in the very character of the club. They would move to a new stadium in the suburbs and suffer various misfortunes. In the mythological sense, it almost seems that had an unfortunate, easily avoidable incident at Washington's Shoreham Hotel not happened, the "Camelot" nature of the Angels might have been allowed to live on.

On August 11, 1964, Belinsky lost a game at Dodger Stadium. He was the victim of poor defense, and after the game Associated Press reporter Charlie Maher found him to be discouraged and distraught over his performance. He was having a season worthy of a 20-game winner, but without better support he was more likely to be a .500

pitcher. It was a crucial point in his career, and telling of the "new Bo." He now took the game seriously, had a chance to make some real money at it, and did not want to let the opportunity of a life-time—heretofore a fantasy in his mind—slip away.

Belinsky poured his heart out to Maher, who wrote a national story quoting the southpaw as depressed over his team's poor play behind him, unhappy with his own performance, and contemplating retirement. Maher pointed out that Bo's words needed to be taken with a grain of salt, coming on the heels of an emotional defeat in the dog days of August, but it all made coast-to-coast headlines.

The Angels and the press corps covering them boarded a plane owned by the Dodgers, which they rented for road trips. A nine-hour flight to Washington, D.C., ensued. One of those writers was Braven Dyer, the 60-year-old dean of the L.A. sporting scene.

TRIVIA

The Angels players were once invited to Eddie Fisher's birthday party at the Coconut Grove. Where was the Coconut Grove?

Answers to the trivia questions are on pages 189–190.

Dyer, who wrote for the *Los Angeles Times*, had seen it all. His vivid descriptions of the "Trojan Wars" with Notre Dame and in the Rose Bowl elevated Southern California football into the realm of myth and lore. He was of a time past and never took to the likes of Bo Belinsky, who in his mind was a playboy of dubious character, holding out for money he did not deserve; a recalcitrant who failed to realize how lucky he was.

Dyer could pull a cork, and by the time the plane arrived in muggy D.C., he was snookered. The players, on the other hand, were kept to a two-drink limit. At 1:30 AM on a hot night, the players dispersed to their rooms. There were no women waiting for Belinsky. Still operating on West Coast jet lag, he and Chance decided they were hungry, taking in a late meal at the Black Steer.

At 3:00 AM they dragged themselves in for the night. Teammate Jimmy Piersall told Bo, "Dyer's looking for you."

Dyer had gotten hold of an East Coast paper with Maher's story quoting Bo about retirement. Fueled by drink, Dyer felt that Belinsky "owed" *him* the exclusive retirement story, not the Associated Press.

The phone rang when they got to their hotel room. It was Dyer, who according to Bo immediately started swearing. A shouting match followed. Belinsky threatened to "put your face in the toilet" if Dyer came near him. Dyer allegedly declared that he was going to come to Bo's room to give him the opportunity.

Chance was taking a bath when Dyer arrived, after having taken his coat off, putting it on the doorknob of the next room and knocking on Bo's door despite a "Do Not Disturb" sign hanging on it.

Dyer stormed in. Bo tried to mollify the old man, who told him, "Go ahead, tough guy, let's see you put me on my ass, let's see you."

With Dyer on him chest-to-chest, Belinsky threw a glass of water on him to "sober him up and make him leave." According to Bo, Dyer reached into Bo's attaché case, pulled out a bottle of hair tonic, and swung it at him, grazing him in the face. Belinsky flattened him with a left hook. Dyer claimed it was Bo who called him and denied he ever swung hair tonic at him.

Dyer fell back, hitting his head on the wall. Blood spurted from his ear and he was unconscious. Chance thought he was dead until they heard Dyer snoring. They called Angels trainer Freddie Frederico, who called Rigney.

Frederico immediately thought Dyer was dying of a fractured eardrum, but he was not hurt seriously, just cut. Rigney arrived and did not believe word one of Belinsky's—or Chance's—stories. The papers got hold of it, and it was big news, complete with photos of old man Dyer in bandages. The public assumed the worst—an old man beaten up by Bo Belinsky.

"Dyer had it in for Bo," said Maury Allen. "He was a crusty, nasty, aggressive person, and he was jealous of him. Bo avoids people like that. You had to 'get' Bo."

An Angel Earns His Wings

Bo Belinsky was traded to Philadelphia, where Gene Mauch had no use for him. He bummed around baseball, in and out of the big leagues, for the next few years. In 1968 he was back in Hawaii, where he made the mistake of throwing a no-hitter. That meant the major leagues came a-calling, and he had to leave paradise.

Bo married Jo Collins, the 1965 *Playboy* Playmate of the Year whose "Vietnam issue" was the highest selling in the magazine's history. Her Marilyn Monroe–style appearance in front of the troops at Black Virgin Mountain was the model for the Playboy-bunny scene in Francis Ford Coppola's *Apocalypse Now*. Belinsky and Collins were a huge item. After a few years away from the limelight, their marriage created more attention than ever. They were happy in Hawaii, green with jealousy in L.A. Divorce was inevitable.

Belinsky retired in 1970, hitting the skids. His interviews with Maury Allen for *Bo: Pitching and Wooing* took place in a Malibu beach pad he shared with a busty hooker who turned tricks by night and catered to his needs by day. Bo's needs consisted of watching soaps and drinking vodka.

The Pat Jordan interview, which became "Once He Was an Angel" in *The Suitors of Spring* and in *Sports Illustrated*, took place over the course of an all-night party and morning hangover session in the Hollywood Hills. It might have been the best human-interest story in the history of sports journalism. Jordan's spot-on descriptions of every detail of the night and its aftermath are nothing less than masterful.

Bo was a guest in the Hollywood Hills pad and tagged along for a trip to the nearby Strip, where they ran into *Playboy* magnate Hugh

Bo's lifestyle caught up with him—he's pictured here "on the town" with starlet Ann-Margret—but he found peace in the end. Photo courtesy of Getty Images.

Hefner. Hefner, who knew Belinsky from his marriage to Jo Collins, invited the group to his Holmby Hills mansion.

Jordan artfully described the party, mostly small-time hustlers, as losers trying to work Hefner for a "score," using their trashy women to sidle up to Hefner, as if their entrées could get him to agree to some nefarious business proposition.

"They tried to hock his silverware," said Bo, who sat off to the side getting drunker and drunker.

Hefner eventually excused himself. The group came to realize it was his way of telling them to get the hell out of his mansion. Back in the hills, Bo exploded at his "friends" for embarrassing him in front of Hef, causing him to break up half the room.

Everybody finally fell asleep. In the morning Belinsky and Jordan resumed the interview, with Bo sniffing the "hair of the dog" in the form of vodka, constantly refilled by his latest squeeze, "a fleshy, attractive redhead" who filled out her bikini as she played bartender and maid.

Bo just called her "babe," and his requests for more vodka were met by an easygoing, "Sure, Bo."

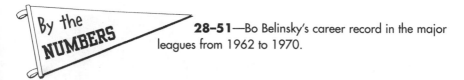

28–51—Bo Belinsky's career record in the major leagues from 1962 to 1970.

Sitting on the nearby couch was a hot teenager in a flowered bikini, painting her toenails.

"Do you like them, Bo?" she asked.

"Sure, babe," said Belinsky.

"She's a stray from the night before," he informed Jordan. "We found her on the Strip. She wants to stay."

Jordan then described the others, still sleeping or "softly moaning, head in hands" scattered throughout the room like "planets occupying their own private orbit." Below the window, two topless chicks lay face up by the pool, burning in the L.A. heat, while two painters worked a few feet away.

"They've been painting that same wall for two days," said Bo.

He gave Jordan boozy nuggets of philosophy, expressing a true love for the *game* of baseball, but not the business of it. The years following the books and articles about Bo Belinsky were not kind to him. At one point he became homeless, living under a bridge. He became a total alcoholic and drug abuser. He lost touch with most of his past associates and had no real friends, other than whatever hooker or floozy still found him charming.

He moved to Hawaii, living the life of a beach bum. Few if any of his neighbors knew he had once been famous (in what is amazing serendipity, he lived next door to this author's cousin, who had no idea who he had been). Then one day he saved the life of a girl drowning in the surf. She turned out to be the heiress to the Weyerhaeuser fortune. She fell for her hero and married him. They eventually did divorce, but it had the effect of helping him get back on his feet.

Bo found Alcoholics Anonymous and blessed sobriety. He moved to Las Vegas, of all places, finding steady work with a Saturn car dealership. That was where this author discovered him in 1994.

In the beginning we had high hopes that Robert DeNiro, who met Bo and told him he remembered the Jersey-raised pitcher, wanted to make a movie about him similar to *Raging Bull.* Bob Case, the Angels clubhouse manager and longtime friend of Bo's, put us in touch with Charlie Sheen, who considered him a role model in a twisted kind of way. We thought the Sheen connection might result in a movie, since he had some clout at the time, but it never happened.

Eventually, we connected with a producing team involving Frank Capra Jr. and Frank Capra III, offspring of the *It's a Wonderful Life* director. The screenplay this author wrote was optioned. Producer Edgar Scherick seemed a good bet at one point, but he passed away. The option expired, and that was that.

Belinsky could be testy. I had my ups and downs with him. It is strange to be around a man you know so much about, when he knows so little about you. I arranged for Bo to conduct some interviews, hoping to generate interest in his story. He appeared with Ralph Barbieri on San Francisco's KNBR, with old pal Bud Furillo when he hosted a show in the 1990s, and with Irv Kaze on the old KIEV.

TRIVIA

Which Angels player was named Most Valuable Player in the 1962 All-Star Game?

Answers to the trivia questions are on pages 189–190.

Bo died in 2001 at the age of 64. His hard lifestyle most likely took 10 or 20 years off his life, but he would have said it was all worth it. What was most encouraging was that, after everything he went through, in the end Bo Belinsky found religion. He was also credited, through prodigious work with the Las Vegas chapter of AA, with saving many, many others from the perilous path he had walked.

The so-called "fallen Angel," who in many ways had inspired this author to find his true calling as a writer, was fallen no more.

The Dean of L.A.

Dean Chance was a cherubic-looking 20-year-old from Wooster, Ohio, who learned painfully in 1962 that a big city could be a lot more inviting than a farm. He was a promising Angels right-hander with a 4–3 record and 3.86 ERA on June 13. After a late-night party thrown for the team by Walter Winchell, he and fun-loving Bo Belinsky were stopped by the cops with two showgirls in Belinsky's convertible. It was 5:00 AM. Chance swore he was "just along for the ride."

"You don't know how close you've come to pitching for Dallas," Bill Rigney told him. "You've got one more chance."

While Belinsky dropped from 6–1 after his no-no to 10–11, Chance was 10–7 from that point forward. Blending a moving fast-ball, a slider, and a change-up screwball, the 6'4", 200-pounder finished his rookie year 14–10 with a sterling 2.96 ERA, both team highs. In September he tossed a one-hitter against strong-hitting Minnesota, and that was a questionable single.

Chance grew up on an 83-acre farm, where his family bred 75 feeder hogs and 60 head of beef cattle. Some people still say he was the greatest prep pitcher in history, posting a 51–1 three-year record with 18 no-hitters at Northwestern High School.

His biggest rival in baseball and basketball was a competitive kid at a rival high school named Bobby Knight. Chance was an all-state basketball star who played five days a week in the off-season to stay in shape. He started to pitch indoors at the local YMCA each January. He was known as a guy who took his time doing *everything*.

"It takes me until June before I really get started," said Chance after his slow-start, fast-finish rookie year.

Chance was a bonus baby with the Baltimore Orioles, receiving $30,000, a sizeable amount in those days. He got his contract right out of high school. This was prior to the June draft, instituted in 1965. Teams could bid for a player, recruiting him the way colleges go after high school prospects without the NCAA restrictions.

"I averaged 28 points playing basketball, and I must have had 25 to 30 college offers," Chance said, "but I chose baseball."

The slow-starting Chance was homesick in the minor leagues, failing to impress the Orioles after three average seasons. He was selected by the Angels for $75,000 in the expansion draft.

"I might have stayed with Baltimore but they had too many pitchers," said Chance. "[Orioles President] Lee MacPhail sent me a real long letter, telling me how sorry he was after Los Angeles picked me in the draft."

Even though Chance and Belinsky were both in the Orioles system at the same time, they did not know each other, only *of* each other. Bo was scarcely a prospect, while Dean was a prize. In the hierarchy of minor league life he was considered part of an elite class. But when Belinsky made the big club in L.A., he achieved his *bona fides.* The Ohio farmboy, with a pregnant wife back home, needed company in the big city. Bo was his tour guide in an "adult Disneyland" during a magical time that has come and long gone.

The 1963 season was a disappointing one. Chance pitched well enough, but the team fell precipitously. His losing record reflected that. Belinsky, of course, was shipped off to Hawaii, breaking up the "Butch and Sundance" routine, as writer Robert Goldman called it in *Once They Were Angels.* But 1964 was a marvel. The Angels continued their lack of effective support for Chance and Belinsky. Chance won 20 but pitched well enough to have challenged for 30, as Detroit's Denny McLain did four years later with support but no more talent.

Chance was similar in physical, mental, and stylistic makeup to the Dodgers' Don Drysdale. They were both tall, lean, and threw hard, using whip-line side motions that ultimately strained their pre-cious arms. Both were mean and willing to work inside.

Mickey Mantle simply gave up trying to hit Dean Chance. He once turned to catcher Buck Rodgers and exclaimed, "This is a waste of time, Buck. I got no chance."

He told writers that, "Every time I see his name on the line-card I want to throw up."

Mantle's France-surrenders-to-Germany capitulation was remarkable, in that he was a league MVP and star of three straight American League champions during Chance's first three years. Furthermore, he was a switch-hitter, meaning he was not forced to face Chance from the right side of the plate where his hard-sinking fast ones and sliders were delivered by way of the box seats along the third-base line.

A more telling explanation of Mickey's attitude is found in what came to be known as "Johnny Grant parties." Johnny Grant was the self-proclaimed "Mayor of Hollywood" (a title in name only; Hollywood being merely a section of the city of L.A. and thus under the jurisdiction of the city's mayor, who in the 1960s was the leg-endary Sam Yorty).

Grant threw wild bashes at his posh house in the hills, inviting all manner of young celebrityhood with plenty of scantily clad women thrown in for good measure. The Angels were said to have suc-cumbed because of too much attendance at these shindigs. The Yankees looked forward to their trips to L.A.—and Johnny Grant parties—like grammar school kids waiting for the last day of school. In *Ball Four*, ex-Yankees pitcher Jim Bouton recalled "treading water in the swimming pool, doing a striptease in my underwear to the theme song of *Lawrence of Arabia* while holding a Martini in each hand" at a Johnny Grant party.

The rumor was that Autry sponsored the parties to tire out the Yankees. The Bronx Bombers would march into boring Cleveland, Detroit, and Minneapolis, mopping up the opposition like Caesar's legions wiping out the last vestiges of Gaul resistance, but they were generally a .500 club at Dodger Stadium, and more like a .000 one vs. Dean Chance!

Chance had only five wins and *four saves* by the 1964 All-Star break, but it included a 14-inning shutout against the Yankees on June 6. That impressed A.L. manager Al Lopez enough to give Dean the start in the midsummer classic. He threw three shutout innings, dominating the great National League hitters. In the second half he was positively "lights out," winning 15 games with eight shutouts, four by 1–0 scores. At age 23 he became the youngest pitcher to win

Some people still say Dean Chance, a farm boy from Ohio, was the greatest prep pitcher in history, posting a 51–1 three-year record with 18 no-hitters at Northwestern High School.

Major League Pitchers of the 1960s

1. Sandy Koufax
2. Bob Gibson
3. Juan Marichal
4. Don Drysdale
5. Tom Seaver
6. Denny McLain
7. Dean Chance (Angels)
8. Jim Bunning
9. Ferguson Jenkins
10. Gaylord Perry

the Cy Young Award, which was given to only one pitcher in baseball instead of to each league's best, until 1967.

Chance and Belinsky were opposites in every way. Chance was the high school phenom, Belinsky a sandlotter. Dean was a rural farmboy, Belinsky a city-slicker. Chance overpowered hitters with heat, Belinsky with a crafty screwball. Chance was a mean, fiery competitor. Belinsky was laid-back even on the mound. Bo knew the country boy could be had. One time Belinsky had one of his girl-friends call Chance in his room from the hotel lobby.

She introduced herself as "Jane...you remember, Jane from Sacramento." Chance responded tepidly, "Oh, yeah. Hi, Jane."

"Jane" then told Dean that she was pregnant, that Dean was the father, and she wanted to know: "What're you going to do about it?"

Chance hung up the phone and raced like crazy to the lobby, where he confronted Belinsky.

"Bo, Bo, I gotta talk to you," he exclaimed.

"What's the matter, Dean?" Bo calmly said. "You look like an expectant father."

Dean blanched. The joke was on him. During one Las Vegas off-season, in which Chance and Belinsky performed some kind of stand-up act, Dean managed to lose $1,500 in between sets. He loved to gamble, but was terrible at it. Another of Belinsky's flames took him for everything he had one night, causing Bo to kick the girl out of the house.

"But he bought her a cab," Dean recalled. "Bo had class."

Chance was traded to Minnesota and won 20 games in 1967, starting his second All-Star Game, a doozy at the brand new Anaheim Stadium, lasting 15 innings before the Americans lost, 2–1. But his sidewinding style was too hard on his arm. He lost his effectiveness in a rapid manner over the next couple of years, retiring after the 1971 season.

Chance was named the pitcher on the A.L.'s All-Decade Team for the 1960s, quite an accomplishment considering Denny McLain won 20 games three times and 31 games one time, captured two Cy Young Awards, an MVP award, and a World Championship.

Chance became an entrepreneur, making money and holding on to his land through good personal times and bad. He maintained his friendship with Bo Belinsky, seeing to it that Belinsky made money at card shows and very likely saving his life once or twice. Like Bo, he experienced a religious reawakening, telling Rob Goldman that he wanted to "forgive everybody. Everybody wants to go to heaven, and that's the stage I'm in."

It would seem that the Angels were aptly named after all.

Little Big Man

Forget Barry Bonds, Ted Williams, Willie Mays, and Joe DiMaggio. Those guys were just baseball players. Albie Pearson never compiled their records, but to some he is a superstar.

Some people know that it is how things *end*, not how they *start*, that counts. In this respect the story of the early Angels, then and now, is telling. It is the story of Albie Pearson.

It was said of American doughboys during World War I that, "Once they've seen *Gay Paree* they ain't gonna wanna go back to the farm no more." The Angels of Bo Belinsky, Dean Chance, Eli Grba, Ryne Duren, Art Fowler, Lee Thomas, and Leon "Daddy Wags" Wagner is the story of wild youth. These were handsome, happy-go-lucky fellows, some just off the farm. They were let loose in the new "Gay Paree"—the Los Angeles of Frank Sinatra and Dean Martin, a time warp of nostalgia and beautiful women wrapped around the art of drinking, which was considered a serious sport at that time.

Some of those early Angels possessed Hall of Fame talent, but none ever made it to Cooperstown. Their lifestyles played no small role in this failure of lost potential. Pearson had no such ability. He took what God gave him and made the most of it.

Over time, the Angels moved to Anaheim and all of their "personality" was gone. Their players drifted into other things, but as the years passed it was Albie Pearson who held them together. In the end, it was the way he lived, not the way they lived, that persevered and meant something when the girls grew old, the lights went out, and the bartenders called "last call." In this respect, the Angels, a

.270—Albie Pearson's lifetime major league batting average.

team whose players made a mockery of their Biblical name and haloed caps, finally earned their wings.

Pearson grew up in El Monte, a nondescript part of the suburban L.A. sprawl. At the time it was semi-rural. At the age of 12 he was 4'4" tall, weighing in at 64 pounds. But his father had been a good football player. His grandfather was a boxer. He inherited their grit and coordination, and in 1958, when he reached 5'5", weighing 140 pounds, he was named the American League Rookie of the Year with the Washington Senators.

A back injury appeared to have ended his career. When the Angels franchise was announced in Los Angeles, Pearson wrote a letter to Fred Haney. He informed him that he had been the Rookie of the Year two years earlier, and that he just wanted the chance to come back to Los Angeles, where he was born and raised, to play ball.

In 1961 Pearson made the club. He was "popular mainly because of my lack of size. I never heard a boo in my life. I was the hero for the guy who never made it."

Little men would come to the park and cheer for Albie Pearson. Little men would write letters saying he inspired them to rise up against meddlesome bosses and nagging wives. Little kids found inspiration in Pearson.

Pearson used every tool at his disposal. He watched opposing teams in batting practice and taking infield, gleaning knowledge on where to play hitters, when to steal bases, how to work counts and spray well-placed singles. He found out if players like Mickey Mantle had too much to drink the night before, using the information to play them in the outfield or take an extra base on them.

Pearson's 1961 roommate was 36-year-old Ted Kluszewski, a few years removed from his years as a feared slugger in Cincinnati. He was still one of the biggest, strongest men in the game. They were a true odd couple, 100 pounds separating them. Pearson was a milk

Local boy Albie Pearson (No. 8) was small in stature at 5'5" and 140 lbs., but he was a big presence for the Angels for many years. Photo courtesy of Getty Images.

drinker while "Big Klu" was a Rob Roy beer man. But they were good friends. Nobody could dislike Albie Pearson.

Not everybody on the Angels was a hellion. Tom Satriano, an impressionable rookie fresh off of Rod Dedeaux's club at USC, was full of the "rah-rah" college spirit. He was a fish out of water surrounded by the hard-livin' veterans, but he was "adopted" by Pearson. Satriano was very moved by the fact that Pearson was "super religious, he never said, 'damn' or 'hell' or anything like that."

According to Eli Grba, however, Pearson had a "little man's complex." Pearson's wife was quite beautiful. One night he took her to dinner, only to get badgered by a patron who insisted on picking on Pearson's size in front of her. Pearson "beat the crap out of him."

Pearson's Christianity was mostly respected but sometimes the source of jokes. One time Leon Wagner and some others secretly followed him around to see if he "walked the walk." He did. Before Wagner died years later, Pearson visited him. It was his example that gave Wagner hope before passing.

Pearson had one vice, however. He owned a "lipstick red" Caddy convertible, just like Bo Belinsky's. One day Bo got a call from one of his minor league flames, an Asian beauty named Zenida, who wore "one of those tight Suzie Wong dresses with the slit right up to her ass." Bo told Zenida to meet him after a night game at his Caddy in the player's parking lot.

Zenida found *Albie's* Caddy and sat herself on the hood, legs twitching all over the place. Albie and his cute-as-a-button wife emerged from Dodger Stadium. Zenida saw Pearson with "this good-lookin' broad," recalled Belinsky, "and figures it's gotta be me, and she's up for a threesome, so she's wavin' at Albie, who's beside himself figuring, 'Why's this Chinese chick on the hood of my car?' And his wife's just pissed."

Belinsky emerged, managing to extricate the little man from that jam, but another time during spring training Bo invited two hotties to the hotel—one for him, one for a sportswriter friend.

"Bo was always spreading the wealth around," recalled Chance.

Belinsky met the two girls, and they were waiting for the writer when Pearson walked into the lobby.

All-Time Best

Angels from Southern California

Position	Name	Location
P	Andy Messersmith	Anaheim
P	Mike Witt	Anaheim
P	Troy Percival	Moreno Valley
C	Bob Boone	San Diego
1B	J.T. Snow	Los Alamitos
2B	Bobby Grich	Long Beach
SS	Rick Burleson	Lynwood
3B	Troy Glaus	Carlsbad
3B	Doug DeCinces	Burbank
SS	Tim Foli	Burbank
OF	Garret Anderson	Granada Hills
OF	Jim Edmonds	Diamond Bar
OF	Albie Pearson	El Monte
OF	Brian Downing	Anaheim
MGR	Marcel Lachemann	Los Angeles
MGR	Gene Mauch	Los Angeles
Broadcaster	Don Drysdale	Van Nuys

"So this one chick thought he was her date," said Belinsky. "Albie's real cute and she just falls in love with him. 'I'm gonna take you home and mother you, baby.' Albie just takes off running, jumps into his car and drives home to his wife in Riverside. He must've called six times to make sure they were gone before he came back."

In May of 1962 Marilyn Monroe visited Dodger Stadium to accept a charitable donation at home plate. There were rumors that she and Bo had interest in each other, which Belinsky slyly neither confirmed nor denied in 1994. Pearson was tasked with escorting Marilyn to home plate. When he met her he saw "obvious sadness and the look of palpable desperation in her eyes," according to writer Rob Goldman, who knew Pearson and interviewed him about it years later.

Pearson felt the need to reach out to Monroe, telling her about the Lord, but the time was not right. He took his position. Shortly thereafter, Marilyn died. Some say she committed suicide, others (ex-husband Joe DiMaggio among them) blame the Kennedys. Either way, Pearson was "tortured" by the "missed opportunity."

In 1963 Pearson finished fourth in the league with a .304 average, but he always had back problems, which eventually ended his career in the mid-1960s. Out of baseball, Pearson became an ordained minister, opening his home and mission to wayward youth. His work took him all over the world, spreading the Gospel and creating a network of ministries.

When Bo Belinsky passed away in 2001, it was Pearson who was with him toward the end. Belinsky had battled cancer for six years.

Albie Pearson stands as a man among men—the biggest of them all.

The Big A

When the newly christened *California* Angels opened play at Anaheim Stadium in 1966, they became the first major suburban sports franchise. Until then teams always played in city centers. This included the L.A. Coliseum and Dodger Stadium, both of which are within close proximity to downtown. Candlestick Park in San Francisco is not located in the heart of the city, but its urban setting was by no means the result of "white flight."

Many believe that Gene Autry saved his franchise by giving them an identity separate from the Los Angeles Dodgers. Orange County, however, is very much identified with L.A. Many commute to the city from the comfortable towns of Newport Beach, Huntington Beach, Anaheim, Fullerton, and Tustin. But over the years the Angels and Disneyland combined to spearhead a growing community that now has its own airport, its own major business and cultural centers, and even its own TV shows, *The O.C.* and *Desperate Housewives*, all of which mythologizes the county as a land of wealth, privilege, and beautiful people.

Autry's bold vision opened the door to outside-the-city stadiums and arenas in Long Island, New York; East Rutherford, New Jersey; and Auburn Hills, Michigan, with plans for more of the same.

Two things inspired Autry to explore Orange County. One was the obvious success of Disneyland, which opened a few years before he acquired the club. The other was a conversation he had with Branch Rickey in 1960. "The Mahatma" congratulated Autry on his purchase and was told that the team would play in L.A., renting Dodger Stadium when it opened in 1962.

"I advise you to get out from under as soon as you can," Rickey said.

That *Los Angeles Herald-Examiner* sports editor Bud "the Steamer" Furillo, who was probably the man most responsible for the great publicity of Bo Belinsky, claims to have come up with the term, "The Big A"?

Rickey pointed out that the Browns were forced to leave St. Louis to the Cardinals; the A's ceded Philadelphia to the Phillies; the Braves left Boston to the Red Sox; and the Yankees had done to the Dodgers and Giants what Caesar had done to Pompeii.

In succeeding years, Rickey's advice proved more or less correct. Los Angeles is such an enormous market that one could say the old rules no longer applied, and the same adage might have been made in regards to the success of the Mets and Yankees in New York City, a city so huge that it could absorb both franchises. But the Mets, not unlike the Angels, occupy a different borough from the Yankees. In the Bay Area, the Bay Bridge separates the San Francisco Giants from the Oakland A's. Washington and Baltimore share separates states. Only in Chicago have two big-league clubs shared a city continuously without the interruption of expansion or franchise upheavals. But Rickey's biggest concern was the renting of Dodger Stadium.

"It just doesn't work," he told Autry.

O'Malley planned from the very beginning to win a war of attrition that would ultimately end in the demise of the Angels. Autry's club would have to live with a "seige mentality."

Angels attendance sagged from a wonderful 1,144,063 in the magical summer of '62 to a paltry 566,727 in 1965. The club struggled that season while the mighty Dodgers won a thrilling world championship.

Prior to the 1965 campaign Autry informed O'Malley that the club would not renew their option on the Dodger Stadium lease, which would have tied them to Chavez Ravine through 1968. This meant they would have to build it, or nobody would come, to paraphrase James Earl Jones in *Field of Dreams*. The Dodgers had treated their tenants as second-class citizens, engendering great disharmony between the two franchises.

The city of Anaheim, knowing that the Angels were not happy with the Dodgers and needed to build a stadium, lobbied hard. Autry was already friends with Walt Disney, who had been urging the building of a stadium near his amusement park, knowing that the two destinations would be mutually beneficial to each other as well as surrounding businesses. Orange County was in the news in 1964. Studies revealed that it was the fastest growing area in the country, part of what came to be known as the "Sun Belt."

At the heart of this was a political philosophy known as conservatism, considered a fringe of the "John Birch Right" until Orange County's votes pushed Barry Goldwater past the favored moderate, Nelson Rockefeller, in the 1964 California Republican primary and later the GOP convention.

Autry, a conservative to the core, friends of Republicans Disney, Ronald Reagan, and Richard Nixon, was enticed by Orange County,

Anaheim Stadium, known as the "Big A," at full capacity on the first day of its opening as the Angels host the San Francisco Giants in an exhibition game on April 9, 1966. The 230-foot-high letter "A," with a halo at its top, served as a scoreboard support.

epicentered by Anaheim, which at the time was populated by orange groves and only 150,000 people. An early hurdle was overcome when Autry told Anaheim Mayor Rex Coons that he did not want to call his team the Anaheim Angels. Coons

TRIVIA

When was the first All-Star Game played in Anaheim?

Answers to the trivia questions are on pages 189–190.

realized that every telecast and dateline would read from Anaheim, giving his town all the publicity they could want. The issue was immaterial to him.

A 35-year lease with the city was signed. A contract was entered into with the Del Webb Construction Company to build a compact, modern, 44,000-seat stadium. The package cost Anaheim about $4 million in land value, a miniscule amount compared to current O.C. levels.

A site was picked out: a cornfield located about a mile from Disneyland, a half-hour's drive south of downtown L.A. on the modern Interstate 5 without traffic (which is more like an hour and a half at rush hour). Freeway construction created a cross section of roads with the stadium as a central destination. Today the 5, the 91, the 57, the 22, and the 605 are all used to get to or connect to the stadium.

It also turned Anaheim into the central hub of the county. Santa Ana is the county seat, home of the civic center, a large junior college, a big sprawling population, and the major newspaper, *The Orange County Register*. Anaheim stole their thunder. Elite coastal enclaves like Newport Beach, Huntington Beach, and Seal Beach were happy to see the stadium built away from their cities. They had enough traffic and tourists in the handling of their beach popularity, enjoying a separate identity from inland Orange County.

The communities around Anaheim all benefited from the creation of the stadium and the movement of the team. These include nearby Fullerton, Yorba Linda, Brea, Placentia, Villa Park, Garden Grove, Buena Park, Cypress, La Habra, and surrounding towns. Certainly smog, traffic, and congestion are problems these places deal with, but property values, tax revenue, and prestige came to them, too.

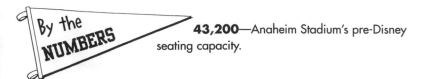

43,200—Anaheim Stadium's pre-Disney seating capacity.

The stadium itself would take on some of the earmarks of Dodger Stadium, in some ways better, in most ways not better. It would be a baseball-only facility with much of the near-field seats intimately closer to the action than Dodger Stadium. Like its counterpart, it would be as clean as a whistle. In terms of style, employees, customer service, and amenities it would take on the scrubbed, white Republican qualities of its surroundings. It would offer expansive parking and access, featuring a giant *A* that symbolized its universal nickname, the "Big A." Unlike Dodger Stadium, it was located on flatlands without the kind of "Hanging Gardens of Babylon" foliage and hills of Dodger Stadium. In this respect it was more utilitarian than the more artistically stylish Dodger Stadium, offering the unfortunate site (on TV even more than in person) of the 57 Freeway beyond center field. While on clear days Saddleback Mountain offers some natural beauty from certain vantage points, this is too often lost to the smog or night games.

Anaheim Stadium, while built for baseball, can, like any facility, be jerry-rigged for football usage. Orange County features the finest prep football competition in America (yes, better than Texas) and has often found it inviting. At the time of its building, sports facilities were commonly multipurpose stadiums (Busch Stadium, Atlanta–Fulton County, Shea Stadium, Oakland-Alameda County Coliseum, Houston Astrodome, and later Riverfront, Veterans, and Three Rivers Stadium). Autry promised the city of Anaheim he would help lure a pro football team to the city, meaning that when the time came he would entertain the prospect of renovating the facility in accordance with this prospect. This would prove to be a mistake.

The 'Burbs

Fred Haney had masterfully handled the expansion draft prior to the 1961 season, mixing a variety of effective veterans with talented youth. In 1966 he lost his touch, this time going for experience and instead getting age in the form of over-the-hillers Lew Burdette (39), Frank Malzone (36), Norm Siebern (32), and Ed Bailey (35).

"We must make a good showing," Haney said at the 1965 winter meetings, "and that constitutes a first-division finish. From the stands we looked dead last year. We have to recapture the spirit and attitude of three years ago."

While it is of course not logical to say this, much of the "spirit and attitude" of '62 seemed embodied in the Sunset Boulevard style of the team and its colorful players. By 1966 the "Rat Pack" mentality of JFK's era seemed gone, replaced by a "strange brew" of protest and bad karma. The team had moved to a place where crewcuts, Christianity, and anti-communism were the dominant sentiments of the day. While these values (well, not so much the crewcuts) would find a national voice again, in the late 1960s the team and its new city looked out of touch.

Baseball was in a culture war in the 1960s. Football was sexy and violent, featuring renegades like Joe Namath and Fred "the Hammer" Williamson. Baseball, particularly American League baseball, was behind the times. David Halberstam would write a book called *October 1964*, in which he used that year's World Series contenders as metaphors for a changing America.

The Cardinals were the new Democrats—brash, young, aggressive; comprised of educated, proud African Americans; Latin Americans; and Southern whites. The Yankees were country club

Republicans in their pinstripes, just waiting for the long ball. The Yankees—like the GOP—would make a huge comeback, but both were down in the mid-1960s.

The club decided to take on the name *California* Angels, which made a certain amount of sense. While Anaheim may be considered a suburb of Los Angeles, it also may not be. After a bad experience at Dodger Stadium, all efforts were made to distance themselves from that image. The Twins had taken on the name of a state, not just a city. Orange County in many ways thought of itself as the most Californian place in California—a little bit of Righteous Brothers (their name birthed by an African American El Toro Marine who, after hearing "You've Lost That Lovin' Feeling," exclaimed "That's *righteous*, brother!") and a little bit of The Beach Boys ("Surf City U.S.A." being Huntington Beach).

Dean Chance, Fred Newman, Buck Rodgers, Jim Fregosi, and Albie Pearson were holdovers from the 1961 draft. Hopeful young players included Jim McGlothlin, Paul Schaal, Tom Satriano, Ed Kirkpatrick, and a huge bonus prospect named Rich Reichardt. Second baseman Bobby Knoop would emerge as a very productive ballplayer. Bill Rigney, ever the chameleon, turned in his flowery shirts and Hollywood shades, assuming a more "Reagan Republican" persona in accordance with the time and place. Ronald Reagan was elected Governor in '66, on the enormous voter strength of Orange, Riverside, San Bernardino, and San Diego Counties, counter-manding the liberal north.

Ross Newhan, the author of *The Anaheim Angels: A Complete History*, offered the opinion that Bill Rigney turned in his best managing performance, "pushing, pleading, cajoling, and maneuvering" the Angels into first-division contention in 1966, despite zero offense and mostly disappointing veteran play.

By 1967 the old was out and the Angels had thrown their lot in with a youth movement. This included the trading of Dean Chance to Minnesota for Don Mincher, Jimmie Hall, and Pete Cimino.

TRIVIA

Of Angel pitchers compiling more than 75 decisions and 500 innings pitched, who has the lowest ERA?

Answers to the trivia questions are on pages 189–190.

By the
NUMBERS
25—The number of home runs hit by Don Mincher in 1967. In '68 Mincher was beaned in the face by "Sudden Sam" McDowell. Mincher hit only 13 that year and was taken by Seattle in the expansion draft following the season.

It was a shocking move to allow a pitcher to go to a contending team in the same league, giving him the chance to "come back to haunt them," as Chance said. In 1967 Chance's 20 victories propelled the Twins into contention for first place until the last day. The Angels, vastly improved, made a run at it, but without a stopper of Chance's ability, did not have enough gas in the tank to stay with the Red Sox, Twins, Tigers, and White Sox in one of the most furious pennant chases of all time.

On Opening Day, rookie Governor Reagan, whose visage may as well have been carved into Saddleback Mountain, Rushmore Style—so popular was he in this neck of the woods—threw out the first ball. The California Angels defeated Denny McLain and the Tigers 4–2.

After that, the Angels dropped precipitously while the rest of the league got down to it, but in June they picked things up. The star was a right-handed Cuban relief pitcher named Minnie Rojas, who was brilliant in setting club records for appearances (72), saves (27), and ERA (2.51). Rojas would become the first player to suffer the so-called "Angels Curse" when he hurt his arm in 1968 and was paralyzed in a tragic car accident in 1970.

The loss of Chance forced Rigney into a utilitarian use of starters and relievers, with Rojas playing the central role. In a league and at a time when pitching dominated, California was third in the junior circuit in 1967 with a 3.19 ERA.

With four teams from the East and the Midwest knocking themselves out, the sole California team (the A's were still in Kansas City) crept up on the rest of the league, pulling to five games over .500 and four and a half games out on July 10. By August 14 they were a game and a half off the pace. Five teams were separated by two and a half games.

Minnesota entered the Big A. The Twins were a talented, veteran club. They had won the American League title two years before. They had power, defense, and pitching. With Chance, they may have been

That the 1967 Angels had a 53–30 record at Anaheim Stadium? But "home sweet home" became "paradise lost" in 1968, when they were only 32–49 at home.

better in '67 than in 1965, when they took Sandy Koufax and Don Drysdale to seven games before losing the World Series.

Star shortstop Jim Fregosi, a warrior with the most competitive juices on the Angels, committed a costly throwing error in a 2–1 Twins victory. After that, Angels bats went as silent as the guns of November 11, 1918. Jim Perry shut them out 4–0 followed by a masterful performance by Dean Chance, 5–1.

Great teams pull themselves out of the hole. The Angels were not a great team. They arrived in Boston with as much confidence as Saddam Hussein's Republican Guard when told to keep the Americans out of Kuwait. Four games: a BoSox sweep. The series ended the Angels' hopes and turned the corner for Dick Williams, Carl Yastrzemski, and Boston, who up to then were waiting for disaster to ring.

But the series was tragic, too. California's Jack Hamilton, a known spitball artist, beaned Boston's promising outfielder, Tony Conigliaro, ending his season. He returned in 1969 and enjoyed great success for two years, but after a trade to California in 1971, he struck out five times in one night against Vida Blue and his bullpen in a 20-inning, 1–0 loss at Oakland. Blaming double vision, Tony C. retired then and there. He seemed to find himself as a California sports announcer, entrepreneur, and ladies man, but died after an untimely heart attack and coma, which many could not help believe was related to the 1967 beaning.

Hamilton was haunted by the beaning and was out of the game two years later. His conscience may have been bothered by the notion that Tony C. was looking for a spitter, which was why he leaned into the inside cheese. Buck Rodgers and the Red Sox, perhaps knowing of Hamilton's grief over the incident, did not assign blame, asserting it was not a spitter gone haywire.

All in all, it was a true Fenway nightmare, with Boston seemingly inspired to win for their fallen comrade in typical "Green Monster" style, 12–11 on Saturday and then a doubleheader sweep on Sunday. In the second game, California blew an 8–0 lead while Dick Williams kicked his team into high gear in a wild argument with umpire Bill Valentine.

After that, it was all over but the shouting. But the image of the Angels as a docile West Coast team unable to handle the pressures of a big-time pennant race was assuaged somewhat when they acquitted themselves with style over the final week.

The exhausted contenders were taking haymakers at each other like Rocky and Apollo Creed. Chicago, who had hung in there throughout on the strength of pitching and defense, finally succumbed. Minnesota with Chance and Detroit with McLain seemed to be the logical favorites with a week left. Both were on the Angels schedule.

First California beat the exhausted Chance and the Twins. Then, on the next-to-last day, Fregosi started a six-run, eighth-inning rally, wiping out a 6–2 Detroit lead, capped by his second hit of the inning, a two-RBI single. The California win had the effect of knocking Detroit out of the driver's seat, forcing them into a must-sweep doubleheader on the final day just to gain a tie.

The next day Detroit won the first game 6–4 at Tiger Stadium. Chance was on fumes, unable to stop the relentless Red Sox at Fenway. With the fall shadows descending on a cold, gray Tiger Stadium, the Angels looked dead again but came from behind a second time on the strength of homers by Reichardt and Mincher. George Brunet saved the game by inducing Dick McAuliffe into a two-on double play to end it for the Tigers. California won 8–5.

Boston, a ninth-place team in 1966 with the least pitching depth (albeit the best ace, Jim Lonborg), was carried by Carl Yastrzemski, putting on one of the great displays in all sports history to lead his team to an "Impossible Dream" pennant.

At 84–77 the Angels finished fifth, seven and a half games back. The spirit and attitude of 1962 had been recaptured, only this time they seemed more youthful, less fluky, and certainly more stable than the wild livers of Sunset Strip infamy.

The New Breed

Something happened to America and to baseball between the innocence of 1962 and war-ravaged 1970. Two black Angels might
symbolize this era.

Leon "Daddy Wags" Wagner was a lighthearted, heavy-hitting
28-year-old reject of the San Francisco Giants and St. Louis
Cardinals, who in 1962 said, "I owe all my success to Iron Mike," a
newfangled pitching machine that was used to turn him into a big
league fielder.

Considered a klutz with the glove, Wagner had worked in 1960
with Cardinals coach Harry Walker, who turned Iron Mike upwards,
shooting balls into the sky. Wagner "got so that looking up, I really
had the point of my nose on the ball all the way up and down."
Walker, he said in 1962, "made me a major league outfielder," but
Walker's protests did not prevent Wagner from being traded to the
Angels in the 1961 expansion shake-up.

In 1961 "Daddy Wags" fielded adequately at Wrigley Field while
hitting 28 homers with 79 RBIs and a .280 average. In 1962 the 6'1",
190-pound left fielder who "never worked out but was built like an
Adonis," according to Albie Pearson, led his team with 37 home runs
and 107 RBIs.

"Rig gave me confidence, letting me play every day," said the left-
handed-hitting Wagner.

Wagner was outspoken, a bit of a rebel. For a brief time he was a
star mentioned in the same breath with great minority athletes like
Willie Mays, Henry Aaron, and Roberto Clemente. He was one of the
first, like his rambunctious teammates, to openly talk about things—
like women, white women, and pleasures of the flesh—that

DID YOU KNOW . . . That Clyde Wright is the father of Jaret Wright, who pitched at Katella High School in Anaheim and was the star pitcher of the 1997 World Series for Cleveland?

heretofore were "off-limits" to black players. The Mickey Mantles of baseball, of course, could philander in a manner that made Teddy Kennedy look like a choir boy.

Albie Pearson recalled one game when Wags asked him to cover anything to his left side. Wagner's breath reeked of alcohol. He could not see the ball, much less catch it, but his talent was such that on that day he managed to hit a home run. Pearson recalled that on the fun-loving Angels of '62, there was no racism. When "Daddy Wags" would engage in racial jokes with teammates, it was all said in a joking manner by smiling faces, leading to harmony, not disharmony.

But between 1962 and 1970 a great chasm was splitting "America the Beautiful." The black athlete had woken up to "the fact that I'm black," according to Alex Johnson. Like Wagner, Johnson lived on the Iron Mike, albeit using it for hitting, not fielding purposes. He would turn it up to full speed and slam line drives from Little League distance in an awesome display of hand-eye coordination. Johnson was at least as fierce a hitter as Wagner (think of Gary Sheffield or Albert Belle). Like "Daddy Wags," he was an outspoken black man. Unlike Wagner, however, he *did not* get along with his teammates, although whether they were white, black, or Latino seemed immaterial in the end.

In between Wagner and Johnson was the Vietnam War, the Civil Rights Movement; and the assassinations of JFK, Malcolm X, Bobby Kennedy, and of course Dr. Martin Luther King Jr. The new breed of black athlete was no longer influenced by Jackie Robinson and "turn the other cheek" pacifism.

Muhammad Ali, Jim Brown, Bob Gibson, Curt Flood, and Dick Allen were examples of this militant attitude. These men had no intention of trying to "please the white man," and in 1970 there were many whites who felt they were way out of line. Of all big-league cities perhaps Anaheim, California, was the least receptive to a man of Alex Johnson's temperament.

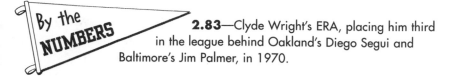

By the NUMBERS 2.83—Clyde Wright's ERA, placing him third in the league behind Oakland's Diego Segui and Baltimore's Jim Palmer, in 1970.

Johnson was obtained from the Cincinnati Reds, where he had been a major offensive threat playing in another conservative town. There was no reason to think 1970 would be special, however. The Angels of 1968–1969 neither hit nor fielded. They featured two stars, shortstop Jim Fregosi and ace pitcher Andy Messersmith, but little else.

Bill Rigney, who had turned down multiyear contracts ultimately worth $200,000 because "I don't want to leave the job undone with the Angels," and "California's still my home," was fired. In 1970 he turned up with the Twins, who had won the West Division under Billy Martin in 1969. It was the last hurrah for Minnesota, a power throughout the 1960s. They would see no glory after winning the division again in 1970 with aging stars.

In Oakland the seeds of dynasty were sown and, by 1970, sprouting. Spurred by the success of the Dodgers, Giants, and Raiders, Charlie O. Finley, rebuffed in his efforts to buy the L.A. franchise in 1960, had transplanted the A's from Kansas City. In Oakland they now represented not just less travel expense for the Angels, but a possible real West Coast rival.

It would have to remain a possibility. Over the next years, Oakland would be a dynasty. Their rivals emerged in Baltimore; in Cincinnati, New York, and L.A. in the Fall Classic; not in Anaheim. The Angels would wonder where they went wrong.

But briefly, in 1970, Alex Johnson's bad attitude was overshadowed by his badass hitting talents on a team that, for the third time in 10 years, showed great promise—for a while.

The Dodgers were rebuilding. Their attendance was down. If the Angels could improve they might catch hold of the fickle L.A. sports heart. Walter O'Malley agreed to a Freeway Series, which the Dodgers swept, but then California won its first five regular-season games, all on the road.

Johnson was with his fourth big-league club. In Philadelphia the presence of Johnson and Allen, who on hot days would play under the shade to avoid the sun regardless of the hitter's tendencies, infuriated the infamous "boo birds."

St. Louis had always been the toughest city for Jackie Robinson to play in. Johnson was bum-rushed out of there faster than you can say, "There's trouble in River City."

It was okay back then to be black in Cincinnati so long as you acknowledged your favorite teams to be the Americans, the Christians, the Republicans, and the Reds...not the Chinese kind. Johnson's favorite team was the Black Panthers. Maybe somebody thought because Anaheim is in California, it was kind of like "nearby" Oakland and Berkeley, where the Panthers and the radicals had turned Cal-Berkeley into the *de facto* staging grounds of American communism.

In Orange County they liked African Americans just fine if they were serving in the Marines over at El Toro or were glamour dolls like Diana Ross. But despite Johnson's *uber*-surliness, the good folks of Orange County came out 1,077,741 strong—up from 758,388 in 1969—to cheer Johnson as he sprayed line drives that made the Big A look like a pinball machine.

Johnson became the first Angel to collect 200 hits. On the final day of the season he went 2-for-3 to beat out Carl "Yaz" Yastrzemski for the batting crown, both at .329 but Johnson better by .003. Johnson immediately claimed racism, stating

TRIVIA

What were considered the best and worst divisions in baseball when they were instituted in 1969?

Answers to the trivia questions are on pages 189–190.

that he had been pitched and defensed hard while Boston's opponents tried to hand the crown to Yaz. Johnson failed to recognize that Yaz, despite his '67 heroics, had through lack of hustle and an attitude that made Barry Bonds look like Red Skelton, squandered more goodwill than France after helping us win the American Revolution, when their imitation of it became instead the Reign of Terror. Yaz was booed at Fenway. His teammates played mean-spirited jokes on him.

Jim Fregosi delivered 16 game-winning hits in 1970. First baseman Jim Spencer hit .274. Second baseman Sandy Alomar contributed 169 hits, 35 stolen bases, and a 22-game hitting streak from the leadoff slot.

However, it was a replay of 1967 when, on September 4, Rigney's Twins entered the Big A. Minnesota repeated the Dean Chance–inspired, three-game sweep of three years earlier. The after-shocks were similar to the '67 four-game debacle at Boston, sans any beanballs. This time the nine-game losing skein cost them second place, which the A's previously seemed willing to hand them.

At 86–76, California could look to injuries (Fregosi, Messersmith, Ken McMullen, Jose Azcue, and Greg Garrett) as legitimate excuses for not coming closer to the 98-win Twins. Messersmith, a pitcher of Cooperstown talents, who for various reasons will never see the Hall of Fame, was reduced to 11 wins but went to the bullpen and was outstanding.

Out of nowhere, southpaw Clyde Wright won 22 games, including a no-hitter, but no one confused his off-field activities with Bo Belinsky, which was fine.

Tom Murphy won 16 and reliever Ken Tatum saved 17.

Purgatory

Never had the Angels looked forward to a season the way they did in 1971. Many prognosticators predicted that they would win the American League West. Minnesota was palpably old. The A's were the obvious obstacle to overcome. While they were a talented crew, they were young and had not proven themselves able to get "over the hump," so to speak. At the beginning of the year, new manager Dick Williams was thought to be too fiery to handle the modern player. Nobody could possibly predict the season Vida Blue would have.

The Angels distanced themselves from their past. Aside from the disappearance of the old-style Angels—Bo Belinsky, Dean Chance, and Bobby Knoop, to name a few—the team's character took on a major overhaul in the form of new general manager Dick Walsh and manager Lefty Phillips. Their philosophies were much different than Fred Haney's and Bill Rigney's.

Walsh, whose nickname was "the Smiling Python," showed his hand when he traded sharp-fielding third baseman Aurelio Rodriguez for the average Ken McMullen. Walsh could not relate to the Spanish-speaking Rodriguez, parting with talent for this reason; an unheard-of move in today's game.

A major trade was supposed to transform the team into a champion. Hard-throwing closer Ken Tatum was traded to Boston for Tony Conigliaro. Tony C. was the toast of baseball. He had made a complete recovery from his 1967 beaning, earning Comeback Player of the Year honors in 1969. In 1970 he was spectacular, knocking 36 homers with 116 RBIs for the Sox. At the time, he had people talking about Babe Ruth's records. Playing at Fenway he seemed powerful enough to hit 61 homers over the Green Monster. He was young enough to appear capable of challenging 714 in his career.

Tony C. was a New England guy, a folk hero in Boston. He looked like a movie star. Women swooned over him. Playing for the Angels, he seemed destined to take Hollywood by storm in one way or another. He moved into a Newport Beach apartment next door to actress Raquel Welch, fueling the fantasies of every male fan and a few female ones.

The Angels were on the verge of taking L.A. from the Dodgers, who were in the middle of a youth movement playing in a division dominated by Cincinnati. Anaheim Stadium was thought to be the best in the league. Older stadiums just looked *old* in 1971. Even Fenway Park did not have the mystique attached to it today. Yankee Stadium, five years from renovation, was crumbling. The Angels looked to be the future.

All of the high expectations, however, were a thin veneer hiding a growing cancer named Alex Johnson. In 1970 Johnson's league-leading batting exploits overshadowed the fact that he accused opponents of favoring Yaz because he was white. He had poured coffee grounds on the typewriter of acerbic Angels beat writer Dick Miller and had exchanged batting cage punches with *his best friend on the team*, Chico Ruiz.

TRIVIA

The year 1971 was probably the worst all-around year in Angels history. What was their one bright spot?

Answers to the trivia questions are on pages 189–190.

He refused to conduct interviews, instead launching into obscenity-laced tirades. However, Alex Johnson was not a comic book character. It would be easy to stereotype him as dumb, or an "angry militant." He was not dumb. His wife was attractive and pleasant, often apologizing for her husband's behavior. Writer Ross Newhan, who covered the team at the time, referred to Johnson as a "Prince Charming away from the park…"

Johnson tried to explain himself once, granting an interview in which he said, "Hell, yes, I'm bitter. I've been bitter since I learned I was black. The society into which I was born and in which I grew up and in which I play ball today is anti-black. My attitude is nothing

A major trade before the 1971 season was supposed to transform the team into a champion. Hard-throwing closer Ken Tatum was traded to Boston for New England folk hero Tony Conigliaro (above).

more than a reaction to their attitude. But they [whites] don't keep their hatred to themselves. They go out of their way to set up barriers, to make dirty little slights so that you're aware of their messed-up feelings."

What Johnson needed was something the Angels did not have. He might have thrived in Oakland, the town and its teams. The "Angry A's" seemed to fuel themselves with their in-house fighting. Another Oakland sports figure, Al Davis, might have been able to harness an athlete of Johnson's Hall of Fame talents, as he did with many "renegades" on successful Raiders clubs.

That Alex Johnson was the brother of Ron Johnson, a running back for the New York Giants?

The Angels broke camp and won a few low-scoring games the first week while Oakland got off to an 0–3 start. Maybe, just maybe. But there was something else amiss: their new uniforms.

The uniforms and caps worn by the Angels from 1961 to 1970 were beautiful in their simplicity. In 1971 the Age of Aquarius had taken its deleterious effect. The old flannel uniform was being replaced by the double-knit, a sleeker look left on its own, but a bad one in the form of pullovers, garish colors, strange designs, odd letter schemes, high stirrups, and other *That '70s Show* oddities. It would not be correct to say that the Angels uniforms of the 1970s were the worst in baseball. The A's, White Sox, Padres, Pirates, Astros, and Braves had them beat. But they resisted tradition, which the Dodgers and Yankees, to their credit, did not.

The scruffy A's were everything that Angels fans could look down upon. They played in a near-empty stadium in a blue-collar city without a semblance of glamour. But while California went into a hitting slump, unable to swing its way out of a paper bag, the A's looked like something from the best of Connie Mack's era. Vida Blue was *spectacular*, and Oakland, featuring other stars like Reggie Jackson, Catfish Hunter, and Sal Bando, had the division wrapped up by Memorial Day.

Tony C. was as disappointing as any player has ever been, setting world records for utter futility. On July 9 at the Oakland Coliseum, the Angels ran into the buzz saw that was Vida Blue, who mowed Conigliario and his mates down like a clear-cut forest. Tony C. never *saw* the "Blue Blazer," going 0-for-8 and whiffing five times. The game went 20 innings, with Oakland winning 1–0.

Nobody really went to sleep after the game, so at 5:00 AM Tony C. called a press conference to announce that he had double vision. His eyes obviously had deteriorated as a result of the beaning. He had to quit, saying that to continue would result in his ending up "in a straightjacket with the other nuts."

By the time Tony C. quit, Lefty Phillips said the "Big A stands for 'agony.'"

Conigliaro, considered a malingerer and clubhouse trouble-maker—as if dark forces had totally replaced his sunny Boston demeanor—just left more room for Johnson's disease to spread. Displaying none of the offensive firepower of his Cincinnati or 1970 days, here was a guy who had gone from a despicable superstar to a despicable .260 hitter with zero power! They always said Stalin could play in the bigs if he won 20, but Bobby Seale popping up with the bases loaded was not going to last.

Johnson got in fights and arguments with everybody. Ken Berry had to be restrained from fighting him. Clyde Wright raised a stool but then figured it would bounce off Johnson and the consequences would not be good for Clyde. He backed off.

But Johnson and the volatile Chico Ruiz went at it every day in a series of hate-filled confrontations. It got so bad that in June, Chico, who at one time had been Alex's only friend until the September 1970 batting cage slugfest, started carrying a gun to the park in case Johnson attacked. Ruiz and Johnson were once so close in Cincinnati that Chico was the godfather of Alex's adopted daughter.

But that was that. *Sports Illustrated* played it like Bonnie and Clyde or "Lepke" Buchalter. The season just played itself out. Johnson was suspended and disappeared from the scene. In the 2000s Robert Goldman, a one-time Angels batboy, tracked Alex down for a great book called *Once They Were Angels.* He compared Johnson to the boxer Sonny Liston, a taciturn man of dubious morality and great ability.

Almost 40 years after that notorious year, Jim Fregosi, who cared only about winning, said that Johnson's bad attitude was "way overblown." Others, like Clyde Wright, still did not want to talk about it.

"I'm ornery to the point of determination, but not evil," was Johnson's assessment of himself given the reflection of time. He still insisted that some writers, Dick Miller in particular, were just plain liars. Wright, no fan of Johnson's, felt that Miller deserved coffee grounds in his typewriter. Ex-teammates tried to be fair,

All-Time Angels Batters

1. Troy Glaus
2. Rod Carew
3. Tim Salmon
4. Reggie Jackson
5. Wally Joyner
6. Alex Johnson
7. Garret Anderson
8. Don Baylor
9. Darin Erstad
10. Brian Downing

characterizing the problems as 50-50 the fault of the club and of Johnson's.

"In essence, I'd agree that I didn't have enthusiasm," Johnson admitted.

Ron Fimrite's "Fallen Angel" piece in *Sports Illustrated* had pointed out that, despite Johnson's protestations over mistreatment of blacks, Ruiz had been quoted by the *L.A. Times* saying, "I'm as black as you, and I hate you. I hate you so much I could kill you."

Johnson theorized that Walsh "turned" Ruiz against him, playing Iago to Ruiz's Othello.

Former Angels pointed out that Johnson probably suffered a mental illness of some kind but did not pick physical fights, just verbal ones, despite the fact that his strength made him the favorite in any battle royales. A psychiatrist had determined that Johnson suffered from "severe reactive depression," but to this day Johnson gives no credence to this notion.

Dick Miller and Dick Walsh did not dispute that racial prejudice was at play with Alex Johnson, stating that the handling of his case by Commissioner Bowie Kuhn and A.L. President Joe Cronin had "overtones of racism."

"When he wasn't in uniform he was one of the nicest guys to be around," Fregosi recalled, echoing Newhan's "Prince Charming" analogy and fueling speculation that whatever disorder was going on, it had to do with the Angels locker room first and foremost. Media coverage came in a close second. Johnson did like Marvin Miller, head of the nascent player's union and in some quarters considered a bigger villain than Johnson.

In the end, like Dean Chance and Bo Belinsky, Johnson found faith to be the "balm of Gilead," healing his wounds. He has five grandchildren and sounds like Bill O'Reilly when he says that the problem with America today is that they "took prayer out of school."

If he had talked like that when he was in Orange County, he might have been elected to Congress instead of getting run out of town on a rail.

The Project

There are many baseball fans who, when asked who the "best pitcher in baseball" is, respond "Nolan Ryan." Throughout the late 1970s, 1980s, and into the early 1990s, the idea that Ryan was the best of all pitchers was a pervasive concept. The truth is, Ryan was the most *dominant* pitcher, but not the best. However, it was in that dominance, that spectacular style of power and heat, that Ryan impressed upon the masses the idea that none was better.

Ryan pitched from 1966 to 1993. It was an incredible career that spanned eras. Contemporaries of Nolan Ryan who are considered greater major league pitchers include Sandy Koufax, Bob Gibson, Tom Seaver, Jim Palmer, Steve Carlton, Roger Clemens, and Greg Maddux.

Long barroom arguments could ensue over whether he was "better" than Don Drysdale, Juan Marichal, or Catfish Hunter, not to mention Rollie Fingers and Dennis Eckersley.

Nolan Ryan was the greatest *strikeout* pitcher in history. He is generally considered to have had the best *fastball* of all times. When he was on, he was as *dominant* as any modern pitcher, with the exception of Sandy Koufax from 1962 to 1966. Of course, Ryan had longevity while Koufax was a "shooting star."

But Ryan was not the man you wanted on the mound Game 7 of the World Series. Koufax, Gibson, or Hunter was. He did not possess the consistency of Seaver or Clemens. When Palmer or Maddux took the hill over the course of many years, the results were almost assured, at least in glorious memory.

When Ryan took the mound, he might strike out 16 or 17 and pitch a no-hitter, but he also might walk seven in a spectacular 3–2

IF ONLY . . . Nolan Ryan had remained in New York and accomplished for the Mets what he did for the Angels, the Mets might have reestablished the greatness of 1969 behind what would have been the most dominant one-two pitching combination ever (Tom Seaver and Ryan). Ryan would have gone down in history as that rarest of true celebrities in the American pantheon: the New York sports icon, a status symbol claimed by a tiny few (Seaver, Babe Ruth, Lou Gehrig, Joe DiMaggio, Mickey Mantle, Reggie Jackson, Frank Gifford, and Joe Namath).

loss. When others were winning 20 games and Cy Young Awards, Ryan was leading the league in walks, completing over 20 games, but losing 16, 17, or 18 games.

While Ryan's best years were in Anaheim, his legend was made in Houston and especially in Arlington, when fans marveled at his ability to throw heat well into his forties. His gentlemanly Texas demeanor made him popular. His friendship with a future president made him a Lone Star legend. But in these halcyon years, when he held elder statesman status, many fans were lulled into thinking none were better. He was winning 16 or 14 or 12, but "the Ryan Express" had everybody mesmerized.

Okay, so Nolan Ryan was not the best pitcher of his era, much less of all time. So what was he? Well, he was an absolute first-ballot Hall of Famer and the finest pitcher in the history of the Angels, not to mention the best pitcher the Astros and Rangers ever had.

Ryan was born and raised in Texas. Because he threw so wickedly hard it might be assumed that as a high school ace he created a legend not unlike Ken Hall, "the Sugarboat Express," whose exploits as a Texas prep football star are said to eclipse all others. Not so, according to Mickey Sullivan, a scout who saw Ryan growing up in Alvin.

"He threw about 86 miles an hour," said Sullivan, who became the head baseball coach at Baylor University.

Ryan was tall and thin. He needed to develop. The New York Mets, baseball's worst team, signed him. His strength came quickly, and with it terrific speed on his fastball. Because the team was so bad, they moved prospects through the farm system quickly. Ryan made his major league debut at the age of 19 in 1966.

The Mets, a laughingstock since 1962, were in the process of stockpiling one of the finest young pitching staffs baseball had seen in a long time. Tug McGraw was another talented hurler. Tom Seaver was signed off the University of Southern California campus and in 1966 was wowing everybody in the International League. Southpaw Jerry Koosman was coming up through the system.

Ryan, the high school kid who supposedly threw 86 mph was by now bringing it closer to 100, but with speed came control problems. He had not perfected his pitching delivery. Footage of him with the Mets shows that he had a high leg kick, a long stride, and a straight

Nolan Ryan hurls the ball in the first inning on August 21, 1974, against the Detroit Tigers. Despite fanning 19 Tigers, Ryan lost in the eleventh inning, 1–0. Ryan struck out 19 batters for the second time in three starts and set a major league record for most strikeouts in three consecutive games—a total of 47.

Hardest-Throwing Pitchers of All Time
1. Nolan Ryan (Angels)
2. Bob Feller
3. Walter Johnson
4. Steve Dalkowski
5. Sandy Koufax
6. Randy Johnson
7. Roger Clemens
8. Tom Seaver
9. Lefty Grove
10. J.R. Richard

over-the-top delivery. Later he would learn to tuck his knee almost to his chin, providing a hesitation that gave him just enough of a pause to gather all his energies before releasing the ball. His arm action with the Angels would be just a bit short-arm, slightly more three-quarter.

Ryan's pitching maturation would be attributed in part to Seaver, whose "drop and drive" style influenced young pitchers on every team he played on, but it took years to take for Ryan.

In 1967 Ryan was sent to the minors for seasoning. He was so wild that the Mets never brought him up. In 1968 he pitched 134 innings and walked 75 batters. Seaver and Koosman were a fabulous one-two combination. The team improved dramatically, and it was felt that if Gary Gentry, McGraw, and Ryan could reach their potential, the Mets would be a contender.

In 1969 everybody did reach their potential—except for Ryan. Seaver had one of the best seasons in baseball history. Koosman was an elite big-league hurler. Gentry and McGraw were fabulous. But Ryan was as wild as a March hare.

Manager Gil Hodges used him sparingly but wisely, bringing him in to scare the bejesus out of the opposition for a few innings or a spot start here and there. The "Amazin' Mets" captured the World Championship. While Ryan was not a star, his brilliant performance in the final game of the playoffs against Atlanta was a winning one in relief.

But 1970 and 1971 were not kind years for Ryan. He was acknowledged to be the hardest-throwing pitcher in baseball and possibly the fastest of all time. Some said he headed an elite list of all-time fireballers that included Rube Waddell, Walter Johnson, Bob Feller, and Sandy Koufax. However, he appeared to be falling by the wayside, his name linked to disappointments such as Steve Dalkowski and Ryne Duren.

The Ryan Express

Prior to the 1972 season, the Angels made a blockbuster trade with the Mets, sending their greatest player, shortstop Jim Fregosi, to New York for Nolan Ryan. Fregosi's production dropped precipitously in the bleak "Alex Johnson summer" of 1971. Ryan, a quiet, unassuming Texan, had not taken to the pressures of New York. After the incredible 1969 World Championship, much was expected of them. Seaver was one of the few Mets who responded to the Big Apple's demands.

Ryan was part of the Angels' rebirth. The Angels had always been a bunch of carousers who treated spring training as a chance to hustle girls by the pool. In Palm Springs in 1972, however, Ryan worked harder under pitching coach Tom Morgan and conditioning coach Jimmie Reese than he ever had. Instead of hitting the bars every night, he instead drove two hours on Interstate 10 to Anaheim, where his young wife Ruth and infant son Reid were staying.

His work ethic paid off. Morgan fashioned Ryan's style, tightening his motion. Ryan was tremendous, striking out 329 hitters in 284 innings with 20 complete games to go with a 19–16 record and miniscule 2.28 ERA. Ryan said that New York manager Gil Hodges and pitching coach Rube Walker had given up on him, but now a star was born.

Then in 1973 Ryan put together the biggest year in the history of fastball aces. He was 21–16 with a 2.87 ERA, tossing 26 complete games. He also struck out the all-time major league record of 383 hitters in 326 innings, breaking Sandy Koufax's record of 382 set in 1965. He threw two no-hit games.

Ryan's last scheduled start was on September 27 against Minnesota. The Twins of Rod Carew, Tony Oliva, and Harmon

Killebrew scored three runs in the first inning, but Ryan settled down and started to strike people out. He needed 16 to break the record. Entering the seventh he had 11, but K'd the side to get to 14, with the spray-hitting Carew going down.

"He was just blowing the ball by people," recalled Carew. "His ball literally exploded. I remember he threw Harmon Killebrew a fastball that was up and in, and his eyes got as big as saucers. He was just unbelievable that night."

The Angels tied the game, but Ryan tore his hamstring. Despite the pain he plugged on in the season finale, trying for Koufax's record. The injury hampered him, and he struggled through the ninth, having tied the record. California failed to score in the bottom of the ninth, leaving manager Bobby Winkles with a dilemma. He decided to stay with the struggling Ryan, who along with the fans wanted the record.

Ryan made it through a scoreless tenth but did not strike anybody out. The Angels did their part, not scoring in their half. In the eleventh, Carew walked and stole second. The crowd booed catcher Jeff Torborg's throw to second, not wanting to take an out that Ryan could use for the record, even if it might cost him the game. Torborg had caught Sandy Koufax's perfect game in 1965, the year he set the record.

Rich Reese came to the plate. Winkles visited the exhausted Ryan. It was decided that this would be his last batter, which would have created a lot of booing had Ryan not gotten Reese on strikes. Ryan got two strikes on him.

"Ryan now has two strikes on Rich Reese," announcer Dick Enberg said. "Two-strike pitch is coming up, Ryan sets, here it is, *swung on and missed!*...Nolan Ryan is the major league strikeout king of all time!...Ladies and gentlemen, we have seen one of the finest young men to ever wear a baseball uniform record one of the most incredible records in major league history; 383 for Nolan Ryan!" Then California scored to give Ryan his 21st win, making it a perfect night.

TRIVIA

Where did the term "Ryan Express" originate?

Answers to the trivia questions are on pages 189–190.

Nolan Ryan fires the pitch that assures him of his 300ᵗʰ strikeout of the season, against the Brewers' Mike Hegan in Milwaukee on August 31, 1974. Ryan set a baseball record by compiling three consecutive seasons with 300 strikeouts.

Jim Palmer of Baltimore won the Cy Young Award, which created some controversy. Palmer won three in his career and was the more complete hurler, but a thorough analysis of both their 1973 seasons reveals that Ryan was at least as deserving. Ryan won 22 games with 367 strikeouts and a 2.89 ERA in 1974. He pitched for California through the 1979 season, leading the American League in

DID YOU KNOW . . . That after Nolan Ryan beaned Doug Griffin in 1974, Griffin was out 50 games but came back? Against the Angels on August 12 at Anaheim Stadium, Griffin singled off of Ryan twice, but Nolan struck out 19 batters in the 4–2 California win. It was his second 19-strikeout game of the year. Nineteen was the major league record, shared by Ryan, Steve Carlton, and Tom Seaver. Roger Clemens eventually broke the record with 20.

strikeouts seven of eight seasons. He pitched four no-hitters for California.

Ryan pitched spectacularly throughout the 1980s with the Astros and continued to be a marvel with Texas from 1989 to 1993. He threw three additional no-hitters to finish with seven in his career, shattering all lifetime strikeout records with an astounding 5,714 and a 3.19 ERA to go with his 324 wins.

The career records for wins, ERA, and of course strikeouts bolsters some arguments that he was the best ever, or the best of his generation. His lack of Cy Young Awards and World Championships works against him, as does his 2,795 career walks.

As a popular athlete, however, he is on one of the truly short lists ever. Ryan was and is a complete gentleman on and off the field. He entered Cooperstown in 1999. His only dark moment occurred in 1974 when he beaned Boston's Doug Griffin with a sickening fastball to his head. Distraught, Ryan called Griffin's house that night. His anguish was accentuated when the Griffin's little girl said, "My mommy can't talk because she's with my daddy in the hospital."

Ryan, a father himself, had to fight a battle that others like Koufax and Walter Johnson fought—the realization that they could kill somebody with their fastball, and that if they were to succeed they would have to pitch inside, anyway. Reportedly, this fear had destroyed Steve Dalkowski, a minor league teammate of Bo Belinsky who some say threw *harder* than Ryan but had his career derailed by alcoholism.

"I'm very proud that I have seven no-hitters and was able to throw four in a three-year span, but I would have to say the fourth one is the most memorable because it tied me with Sandy Koufax," Ryan told Robert Goldman.

Many insist on comparing Ryan and Koufax because of the no-hitters and strikeouts.

"Ryan was a more physical pitcher," said ex-Angels manager Norm Sherry, whose brother Larry was Koufax's teammate in L.A. "He would use his legs and had a lot of drive and put a lot of terrific effort into throwing the ball. Koufax was more fluid and gave less exertion than Ryan."

Sherry could not honestly say that one threw harder than the other, but as a general rule Ryan is thought to be the hardest-throwing pitcher ever. A natural comparison comes between Ryan and two right-handers with similar hard-leg-drive styles, Seaver and the Texas-bred Clemens. While Randy Johnson's makeup is much different, many have determined Johnson to be as close to Ryan as any pitcher in terms of sheer velocity.

Ryan's son, Reid, insisted that the key to his father's success came from their hardscrabble family background. Nolan's parents survived the Great Depression, so work ethic was instilled in him. Ryan never took anything for granted. His cattle business was "his first love," something to fall back on.

Lean Years

Despite Nolan Ryan's great success, the 1970s were lean years for the club. The promise of 1970 gave way to the disastrous Alex Johnson debacle. Oakland dominated the division and baseball, but worse from the Angels' attendance standpoint, the Dodgers made a big comeback.

California may have thought they could do it the way L.A. had done it in the 1960s, with pitching and little else. Certainly Ryan and left-hander Frank Tanana were a formidable combination, but baseball is a team game. The offense, defense, and bullpen fell woefully short of the standards set by Ryan and Tanana.

California went through different managers. Former Arizona State coach Bobby Winkles, who had won national championships in college, proved ill-suited for the professional game. The anti-Winkles, hardnosed Dick Williams was brought in. Williams had won titles in Boston and Oakland.

In 1975 the Angels were so weak offensively that Texas manager Billy Martin said they could take batting practice in a hotel lobby and not break anything. Boston pitcher Bill Lee seconded the notion, suggesting that "not even the lobby chandelier would be in jeopardy."

Williams made the biggest mistake of his career, mocking his team by having them take BP in the lobby of the Sheraton-Boston with whiffle balls and plastic bats.

That afternoon, Lee shut them out 6–0.

"He popped off and backed it up," Williams said of Lee. "He embarrassed the hell out of us."

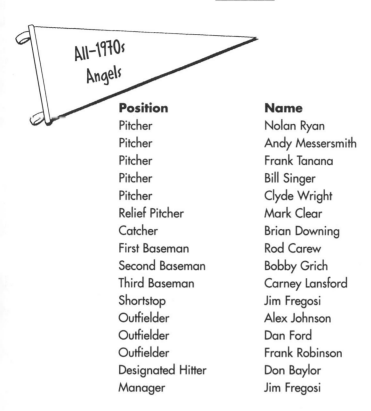

Position	Name
Pitcher	Nolan Ryan
Pitcher	Andy Messersmith
Pitcher	Frank Tanana
Pitcher	Bill Singer
Pitcher	Clyde Wright
Relief Pitcher	Mark Clear
Catcher	Brian Downing
First Baseman	Rod Carew
Second Baseman	Bobby Grich
Third Baseman	Carney Lansford
Shortstop	Jim Fregosi
Outfielder	Alex Johnson
Outfielder	Dan Ford
Outfielder	Frank Robinson
Designated Hitter	Don Baylor
Manager	Jim Fregosi

But Frank Tanana was spectacular. For several years he made a strong on-field argument that he, not Ryan, was the true ace of the staff. He threw a few miles per hour slower, but not by much. He possessed pinpoint control, a great curve, and mound moxie. In 1974 Tanana won 14 games as a rookie. In 1975 he was 16–9 on a team that did not hit, leading the league with 269 strikeouts (including 17 against Texas on June 21), all wrapped around a 2.62 ERA.

Tanana's father was a Detroit police officer. He was California's first pick in the 1971 draft. Tanana was a cocky lefty who reminded everybody of Bo Belinsky, except that he had far more ability (not that Bo lacked talent).

He was cocky as all get-out, stating that, "My idol as a kid was myself. My ambition is to become the best pitcher in baseball. I may have already achieved it."

It seems hard to believe that the team was so mediocre, what with Tanana and Ryan in the same rotation. Ryan was still at the top of his game, throwing a 1975 no-hitter against Baltimore and coming within three and two-thirds innings of duplicating it the next week.

Hope that their offensive woes would be put to rest were kindled in 1976 with the addition of Bobby Bonds, a native of nearby Riverside. Bonds was beset by injuries and contributed little outside the cocktail lounges. Tanana was again spectacular, going 19–10 with a 2.44 ERA.

Tanana's Belinsky-esque reputation was made via his matinee idol good looks and way with the ladies. He lived in the Newport Beach area and was known to frequent the hot clubs there. Beautiful,

Despite masterful performances by Nolan Ryan—shown here as he leaves the field at Anaheim after pitching a no-hitter against the Baltimore Orioles on June 1, 1975—the 1970s, as evidenced by the mostly empty upper deck in the background, were humdrum years for the Angels.

tanned Orange County girls flocked to the Big A, which male fans registered no complaint about. He apparently had a "black book" of some repute, and his exploits on the road were recalled as being on par with Belinsky's.

TRIVIA

When did people begin speaking of an "Angels Curse"?

Answers to the trivia questions are on pages 189–190.

The Sporting News featured a long article on him in which he rated the best American League cities in order of the "talent level" of its female citizenry. The Anaheim–Los Angeles area was at the top of his list, with Dallas and New York drawing his consideration. Oakland was his least favorite.

In 1948 the Boston Braves won the National League pennant behind the pitching of Johnny Sain and Warren Spahn. Writers said their strategy was "Spahn and Sain and pray for rain." Dave Distel of the *Los Angeles Times* dubbed the Angels: "Tanana, Ryan, and a lot of cryin'."

In 1976 Williams and broadcaster Don Drysdale visited Gene Autry in his hotel suite at New York's Waldorf-Astoria. Behind General Manager Harry Dalton's back they suggested Dalton be fired, with Drysdale to take Dalton's job. Autry, a man of loyalty, reacted negatively.

Norm Sherry took over as manager in 1977. The team was favored to win the West Division. Aside from Ryan and Tanana at the height of their game, the club improved themselves through a new concept: free agency.

The Oakland dynasty was broken up by that very free agency. Charlie O. Finley did not have the money to pay his players, so they were scattered to the four winds. Reggie Jackson and Catfish Hunter were now with the Yankees.

Autry signed Joe Rudi, a stellar Oakland outfielder. Don Baylor came in from Oakland, and Long Beach–bred Bobby Grich came from Baltimore. With the Dodgers established as favorites in the senior circuit, talk of a Freeway Series was in the air, and not the preseason exhibition kind.

"I always felt our biggest competition was [Dodgers broadcaster] Vin Scully," said general manager Buzzy Bavasi, a longtime Dodgers

By the
NUMBERS
21—The number of years Ron Fairly played in the major leagues. In his last big-league season, Fairly batted .217 for California. Fairly prepped at Long Beach Jordan High School, was an All-American at USC, an All-Star for several teams, and a longtime broadcaster, including a stint with the Angels.

executive before moving to Anaheim. "We couldn't put anybody on the field as popular as Scully."

Bavasi felt that because of this the team needed "marquee names" that could draw fans, whereas the Dodgers fan base, like loyal USC alumni, stuck with their team through thick and thin. Over the years this has proven to be true; the Dodgers and USC own L.A., while the Angels, Lakers, Clippers, Sharks, Kings, and Bruins, while often excellent, exciting, and popular, tend to deal with the shifting sand of sentiment.

While the addition of Baylor and Grich was believed to add offense, defense, leadership, and a "winning attitude," the biggest mistake was that Autry, despite spending $5.2 million, did not go after Oakland relief ace Rollie Fingers. After Ryan and Tanana, the staff was suspect, especially late-inning relief.

Baylor said the team lacked a "major league attitude," blaming the "laid-back Southern California atmosphere." This is a charge that has been made many times but does not hold up under scrutiny. Southern California produces the most big-leaguers, who seem to develop despite the temptations of beaches and girls. The "SoCal attitude" did not prevent the Dodgers from being the best team in the National League for two decades (the 1960s and 1970s). It certainly did not prevent John Wooden's basketball dynasty at UCLA or the juggernauts of John McKay, John Robinson, and Pete Carroll at USC.

Any hope for 1977 success ended when Tanana was injured. Signed to a new $1 million contract, at midseason he was 10–2 with a 1.84 ERA; the best pitcher in baseball. But he pitched 14 straight complete games, inflaming his triceps tendon. A sure All-Star Game starter, he was replaced by Ryan, who infuriated manager Billy Martin by bowing out in favor of...the beach.

Tanana didn't pitch an inning after September 5 and was never the same again. He finished with a 15–9 record with a 2.54 ERA. The "next Sandy Koufax" would go by the wayside. He pitched for five more teams. In fact, his intelligence and knowledge of the strike zone allowed him to compete in the big leagues as a control artist. For those who saw him once dominate a game like few others, it was a sorry sight, however.

He never approached the Hall of Fame career he could have had.

"Yes, We Can!"

In 1978 the Angels continued to spend Gene Autry's money, acquiring hard-hitting Lyman Bostock, who averaged .323 and .336 in Minnesota the previous two seasons. The $2.2 million he received seemed beyond belief at the time, such was the increase of salaries within a few short free-agent years.

Bobby Bonds was let go, even though he could still hit. He also liked to pull a cork. Bostock, unaccustomed to big money (the Twins had been paying him $20,000), tensed up, opening the year in a terrible slump. In one of the greatest acts of righteousness in the history of sports, Bostock offered to play without pay until he started to perform.

Autry appreciated the gesture but would have none of it. Bostock eventually did pick his average up, but during a road trip to Chicago he was shot dead while sitting in his car. His sainted image was tainted somewhat by the fact that his killer was the jealous husband of a woman he may or may not have been seeing. His agent, who created a bad insurance policy that left Bostock's widow paying enormous tax penalties, tried to extort money from Autry, who summarily ordered all players represented by that agent to be traded or gotten rid of.

In 1978 Brian Downing came to California in a trade with the Chicago White Sox. A product of Magnolia High School in Anaheim, he would blossom. He and teammate Lance Parrish also would be credited with popularizing the weight-training craze that would take over baseball, lasting into the "steroid era."

The Angels drew 1,755,386 fans in 1978, an excellent draw by the day's standards. The Dodgers reached the 3 million mark in winning

The great Frank Tanana had not injured his arm, he would have been one of the greatest pitchers of all time; a Cy Young Award winner, and very possibly a Hall of Famer. As great as Nolan Ryan was, Tanana had the potential to be better.

back-to-back National League pennants. It was a period of great fan excitement for most of Southern California's pro and college sports teams. The USC Trojans won national championships in football and baseball. UCLA did not win the NCAA basketball title, but the imprimatur of dominance still clung to the program, the last vestiges of John Wooden's impact on the program. The Rams were division champions in the days prior to Joe Montana lifting the 49ers into the top position.

Despite the Angels' continuing disappointments on the field, free-agent acquisitions, a strong sense of love for Gene Autry, and good marketing had helped the team capture the Orange County fan base. It was a time in which Southern California seemed to be the center of the sports universe in more ways than one. Many franchises were not doing well, playing in broken stadiums. Anaheim Stadium was a gleaming structure; the L.A. fan was perhaps fickle and late arriving, but willing to spend his sports dollars.

In 1979 the team was expected to capture the West. They had managed to finish strong in 1978, after the death of Bostock, although not strong enough to defeat the Kansas City Royals. In 1979 Jim Fregosi was at the helm. A longtime favorite of Autry's, he had always been thought of as the "future Angels manager." That time was now.

Fregosi was a man's man, a leader. His first order of business was to convince Don Baylor, a designated hitter, that he would be given every chance to play in the field, that the first priority was to the club, and that regardless of whether he was a DH or not, Baylor was needed as a run-producer and example.

Baylor stopped asking for a trade, respecting Fregosi for his up-front demeanor. Dan Ford was brought in from Minnesota, along with Rod Carew, who manager Gene Mauch said was "the best hitter in baseball" as he flirted with the .400 mark on occasion. Second-year

Lyman Bostock was signed and expected to help make the Angels a serious contender in the 1978 season.

third baseman Carney Lansford was a fabulous player; he hustled, played good defense, hit, and never complained.

The Big A drew 2,523,575 fans in 1979, echoing Fregosi's exhortation, "Yes, we can!" It was an offensive fireworks display night after night. They batted .282, their 866 runs averaging 5.3 per game.

Baylor blossomed into the league MVP with 36 homers, 139 runs batted in, 22 stolen bases, and a batting average of .296. Ford drove in 101 runs. Grich hit 30 homers and drove in 101. Lansford added 19 homers while hitting .287. Willie Aikens batted .280 with 81 RBIs. Carew hit .318.

When Ryan saw Downing for the first time after the catcher spent the winter pumping iron, he asked him, "How come you're wearing your chest protector under your shirt?" The muscular Downing, who had not been a star in high school, was one now. He batted .326.

"We just pummeled everyone," said Baylor. "Every day we went to the park, we had it in our minds that we were going to win."

"He was the enforcer," Carew said of Baylor. "He wasn't a loud-mouth or anything. He'd pick guys up in a professional way."

It turned out to be a wild pennant race. Baseball fever engulfed Orange County, indeed all of L.A., but it was all about the Angels. The Dodgers had a losing year.

With a team ERA over 4.00, with Ryan a notch below his mid-1970s form and Tanana a shell of his old self, the team relied on hitting, but the crowd never left games early, always figuring a late-inning rally was in the works.

They trailed by four and a half, then led by five. Kansas City roared back from 10½ games back on July 19 to half a game up on August 31, but when California beat Cleveland in typical 9–8 fashion, they regained a lead they never relinquished. Closer Mark Clear was outstanding in the first half, although he struggled toward the end.

On September 17, California entered Royals Stadium for a four-game showdown with three-time West Division champion Kansas City. The Angels led by three, so the prospects were essentially either collapse or victory. At first it looked like a collapse when Kansas City won two of the first three. Then Gene Autry sent Jim Fregosi a tape of Royals owner Ewing Kauffman telling a Palm Springs radio station that he did not care who won the division, so long as it was not the Angels. Kauffman's beef was with Autry's free-agent spending.

Fregosi played the tape to those very free agents, who, of course, were all rich because of free agency. Therefore, they were big fans of it. In a game typical of the 1979 season, California responded with a high-scoring effort, winning despite shaky pitching by an 11–6 score.

It was neither collapse nor Gettysburg-style decisive victory, but it was enough to swing the season to California. Kansas City came to Anaheim, and Tanana—by now nibbling corners with soft stuff—beat them 4–1 at the Big A.

"For us to win and for me to pitch the clincher," he said, holding a bottle of bubbly, "well, hell, it's unbeliev-able. I've never been this happy. It's like a script. It takes some of the sting

TRIVIA

What did the Angels do to celebrate the 1979 American League West championship?

Answers to the trivia questions are on pages 189–190.

866—The American League–leading amount of runs scored by the 1979 Angels.

out of all the B.S. I've had to go through this year, out of all the frustration of the last six years."

The moment, however, belonged to Autry. Perhaps baseball's most beloved owner, he had waited seemingly forever for a championship. He had paid for it in the form of high-priced free agents. He toured the clubhouse with his friend, former president Richard Nixon.

Nixon, born in Yorba Linda, had resigned his office five years earlier, taking exile and pardon in his San Clemente beach mansion. In the intervening years, he had written a best-selling autobiography, but his frequent attendance at Anaheim Stadium was part of a calculated strategy aimed at rehabilitating his public image. Ultimately Nixon's plan worked, and he would eventually attain "elder statesman" status.

Autry, a conservative reflective of his Orange County fan base, welcomed Nixon who, over the course of the season, became the team's biggest fan. He accompanied Autry through the champagne-swilling celebration.

"I imagine he's 'bout as happy right now as he can remember being," Nolan Ryan observed of Autry. "There's been more spirit on this club than any I've ever been associated with. These guys never knew when to quit. We didn't have any real cheerleader types, but we had a lot of guys who wanted to win."

At 88 victories, the Angels were hardly a team for the ages. It was their best record but not a wild improvement over the 1962, 1967, or 1970 clubs. Now lay the formidable Baltimore Orioles, winners of 102 games. Manager Earl Weaver's team had depth and fabulous starting pitching. They were heavily favored not just to win the playoffs but to defeat whatever National League club faced them in the World Series.

The playoff opener featured the classic confrontation of Ryan vs. Jim Palmer. These were the two preeminent American League pitchers of the decade. In 1973 Palmer had beaten out Ryan for the Cy

Young Award in what many called "East Coast bias." Palmer was on his last legs. Health problems derailed his great career and would stop him shy of 300 lifetime wins, but his experience made him Weaver's choice for the opener. Baltimore's real ace was the 1979 Cy Young winner, Mike Flanagan.

It was not exactly a pitcher's duel for the record books, but Ryan and Palmer battled each other at Memorial Stadium. Both were out by the tenth inning when Baltimore won it, 6–3, on a home run by John Lowenstein. With Ryan gone, California had played their strongest hand. Baltimore stormed to a 9–1 Game 2 lead, but Angels bats could not be contained. California roared back to make it a one-run game before Don Stanhouse stopped the improbable rally and preserved a 9–8 victory.

The Angels boarded a plane for the flight home. Broadcaster Don Drysdale, a sweetheart of a man except when his competitive juices were flowing, accused injured pitcher Jim Barr of malingering. The two sides had to be broken up. Later Drysdale apologized.

With the season hanging in the balance, California scored twice in the ninth on the weak Baltimore bullpen to capture a 4–3 win, giving the Anaheim fans something to cheer about. The next day they faced Scott McGregor, a lefty who was a longtime nemesis of theirs.

McGregor was a teammate of Kansas City star George Brett at El Segundo High School when the program was the best in the state. McGregor had set a California prep record of 51 career victories, and in 1979 he was in his big-league prime. The Angels bats were silent in the face of his big curve, tough sinker, and tight control, slinking home for the winter in the face of Baltimore's 8–0 triumph.

Perennial All-Star

When the Angels of the 1960s were known for their skirt-chasing, hard partying, and 5:00 AM run-ins with the Los Angeles police, Jim Fregosi gave them pure on-field respectability.

They had other good players, of course. Dean Chance was their first superstar, but he was one of those guys associated with run-ins with the cops and was traded in his prime. Fregosi was a perennial American League All-Star, the best shortstop in the league—and probably all of baseball—for the decade of the 1960s.

When Fregosi broke in, shortstops were generally small and wiry. They were expected to be steady defensively, draw walks, hit singles, and steal bases. Fregosi and Chicago's Ernie Banks were exceptions, both providing power at the plate. Fregosi contributed 18 homers in 1964 and 22 in 1970 during an era dominated by pitching. Later, shortstops like Cal Ripken, Alex Rodriguez, Miguel Tejada, and Nomar Garciaparra eclipsed previous power numbers for shortstops (Banks switched to first base in 1962).

Fregosi played in the 1964, 1966, 1967, 1968, 1969, and 1970 All-Star Games. He was named to *The Sporting News* All-Star team in 1964 and 1967 and earned a Gold Glove in '67.

Fregosi grew up in blue collar South San Francisco, a town heavy with Italian influence. Baseball was huge in the San Francisco area. Players like Lefty O'Doul, Tony Lazzeri, and Joe DiMaggio were heroes on the West Coast. They were big influences for Fregosi. He prepped at Serra High in San Mateo, and helped to establish it as one of the great high school sports schools in America. USC and L.A. Rams coach John Robinson went to Serra. Later, Pittsburgh Hall of

TOP 10
All-Time Greatest Shortstops

	Player	Team
1.	Alex Rodriguez	Seattle, Texas, New York Yankees
2.	Honus Wagner	Pittsburgh
3.	Cal Ripken	Baltimore
4.	Derek Jeter	New York Yankees
5.	Ernie Banks	Chicago Cubs
6.	Miguel Tejada	Oakland, Baltimore
7.	Nomar Garciaparra	Boston Red Sox, Chicago Cubs, Los Angeles Dodgers
8.	Luke Appling	Chicago White Sox
9.	Pee Wee Reese	Brooklyn
10.	Jim Fregosi	California, New York Mets

Famer Lynn Swann, Giants superstar Barry Bonds, and New England quarterback Tom Brady, among others, came out of Serra.

Fregosi was signed out of Serra by the Boston Red Sox but was selected in the expansion draft by the Angels. He came up in 1961 and 1962, finally sticking when he batted a solid .287 in 1963. By 1964 he was the premier shortstop in the league, prompting arguments in the Southland over who was better: Fregosi or the Dodgers' Maury Wills.

What set Fregosi apart, according to ex-teammate Eli Grba, was his "fire in the belly."

Ultimately, it was the difference between Fregosi and some of his fun-loving teammates, who often frustrated competitive manager Bill Rigney. Rig could always count on Fregosi. Fregosi was "old school," just like his father, who was said to have been a great ballplayer in South San Francisco but had to go to work to support a young family.

Today, players fraternize and, because of trades and free agency, are often opponents one year, teammates the next. Fregosi did not buy into that way of thinking. He despised Rod Carew after he took Bobby Knoop out with a hard slide. Later, when Fregosi was Carew's manager in Anaheim, the relationship was strained because of it.

"We were both scared rookies when I first met Fregosi in '61," said Tom Satriano. "I didn't see him again until 1963, and I couldn't believe the transition. He had become the backbone of the team."

Fregosi "played like a kamikaze," said Lee Thomas.

"When the chips were down and we needed a clutch play in the field, Jimmy would come up with it," said Albie Pearson.

Rigney recognized early on that Fregosi had managerial abilities, often pulling him to the side to point things out that he would someday need to handle the job.

"Bill Rigney taught us how the game operates, but he also taught us a love of the game that never left," Fregosi recalled.

Jim Fregosi was the best shortstop in the league during the 1960s. Photo courtesy of Bettmann/CORBIS.

In 1964 Fregosi displayed power, batting .277 with 77 RBIs. He and second baseman Bobby Knoop became one of the top double-play combinations in baseball. Fregosi repeated the .277 average in 1965. In the 1967 pennant-chase season he hit .290, desperately trying to keep his club in the race until the end. He led the American League in triples with 13 in 1968, and was probably at his best in 1970.

TRIVIA

Why was Angels general manager Dick Walsh nicknamed "the Smiling Python"?

Answers to the trivia questions are on pages 189–190.

Keeping the club sane in the face of Alex Johnson's shenanigans, he hit 22 homers with 82 RBIs. He played all 162 games in 1966, and three times played over 160 games. He always answered the call.

While Fregosi was considered a team leader, "set apart" from his teammates, he was also single and fun-loving. He was no monk. Albie Pearson, who did live like one, was close to him at first but eventually Fregosi fell in with the party crowd.

He had a "wild hair, yet when I say that I don't mean it in a negative way," said Pearson.

Grba, who loved the nightlife, said that he would be "hustling" a girl when the handsome Fregosi would approach. After that, the focus was all on Fregosi.

All the air seemed to have been taken out of Fregosi when he was traded to New York for Nolan Ryan, a move Autry hated making, but which ultimately proved a good one in that it brought the "Express" to California.

By the time Fregosi was hired to take over as the club's manager in 1978 he had matured, learning the many lessons of a long career, including those imparted to him by Rig. Autry had first thought of Fregosi as a future manager in the 1960s, and his vision proved to be a good one when the 1979 West Division title was won. His constant phrase, "Yes, we can!" became the team's slogan.

"I'll never forget Gene's eyes when I saw him after the game," Fregosi said. "It was as if a black cloud had been lifted from his head forever."

The Great Anaheim Offensive of 1982

In 1980 the air was taken out of the Angels when the great Nolan Ryan signed a free-agent contract with the Houston Astros. Ryan had proposed a contract offer prior to the 1979 season, commensurate with the new free-agent marketplace.

Buzzy Bavasi and Gene Autry, having spent big money to build a contender, miscalculated the situation. Ryan was still dominant, but his statistics were slightly down from the mid-1970s. They felt that he might not have that many more years left. They decided that they would try and negotiate at midseason, which Ryan did not want to be distracted with.

By the All-Star break, Ryan was pitching well and the team was positioned to win their first division. But it was also well established that he could become the richest pitcher in baseball history. The Angels offer, while matching Ryan's original demands, was well below what Nolan now knew he could get.

Autry made what he called "my biggest mistake," which was not meeting Ryan's demands. In truth, Ryan was enticed by the prospect of going home to Texas. He threw a no-hitter in 1981 while leading Houston to the playoffs and continued to dominate for years after that.

The loss of Ryan set the Angels back. In 1980 Kansas City won the pennant. In 1981 "Billy Ball" resurrected baseball in Oakland. By 1982, however, they were poised to take the brass ring.

Fregosi, an Autry favorite, was unable to prod his charges to their 1979 level, but without Ryan or much of a staff, he lacked the tools. He was fired. In came Gene Mauch. Mauch came out of Fremont High School in L.A., which has produced more major league players than any other.

Baseball great Reggie Jackson poses with Angels owner Gene Autry during ceremonies on January 26, 1982, officially announcing that Jackson signed with the Angels in Anaheim.

In looking up the word "intense" in *Webster's*, a picture of Gene Mauch should accompany the definition. A journeyman big leaguer, he took over as the youthful manager of the 1961 Philadelphia Phillies, one of the worst teams in history. Three years later, he had the Phillies in first place with 10 games to go, but panicked. Pitching aces Jim Bunning and Chris Short wore out and the club fell to St. Louis. Lost in the disaster was the fact that Mauch had pushed a decent team well beyond their capabilities.

Many did not get along with Mauch. Controversial players Dick Allen and Alex Johnson did not. Mauch had nothing nice to say to Bo Belinsky when he came over after his banishment from L.A. in the wake of the Braven Dyer incident. In Montreal and Minnesota, Mauch pushed mediocre clubs into occasional semi-contention.

Sparky Anderson called him the "smartest manager" ever, a point Mauch did not dispute. He told Angels beat writer Ross Newhan that the press corps was not "smart enough to analyze me." Mauch was as hard-working as any manager has ever been, a "light-bulb, as explosive as six sticks of dynamite in a bouncing truck," according to Pulitzer Prize–winning columnist Jim Murray of the *L.A. Times*. No aspect of the game escaped his attention, causing him in the estimation of some to over-manage.

"I don't know everything there is to know about baseball," Mauch said in 1982, "but there isn't anyone who knows more."

After 20 years managing also-rans, Mauch was tired of being the "smartest" manager in the game with no championships to show for it. He insisted that Autry and Bavasi provide him with "an influx of winning people." Otherwise, he was satisfied to retire to Rancho Mirage and a sunset of golf and relaxation.

Bavasi met Mauch's challenge, loading California with one of the best offensive teams in history. On the mound, California was lacking the kind of stoppers Mauch had in Bunning and Short at Philadelphia, or that Fregosi had with Ryan in 1979. But the team seemed to have been made complete when Bavasi made a midseason trade for Tommy John, 10–10 and considered expendable by the New York Yankees.

Southern California is well-regarded for producing greater ballplayers than any other area. Bavasi took advantage of free agency and other means to bring in what may be the best SoCal team ever assembled. Doug DeCinces (.301, 30 HRs, 97 RBIs) returned home to play third base, as did catcher Bob Boone. Tim Foli, who hailed from the San Fernando Valley, replaced Rick Burleson (who had played at Cerritos J.C.). Second baseman Grich was

TRIVIA

Which unique major league record is Bob Boone part of?

Answers to the trivia questions are on pages 189–190.

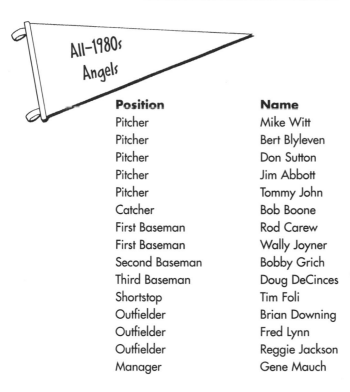

Position	Name
Pitcher	Mike Witt
Pitcher	Bert Blyleven
Pitcher	Don Sutton
Pitcher	Jim Abbott
Pitcher	Tommy John
Catcher	Bob Boone
First Baseman	Rod Carew
First Baseman	Wally Joyner
Second Baseman	Bobby Grich
Third Baseman	Doug DeCinces
Shortstop	Tim Foli
Outfielder	Brian Downing
Outfielder	Fred Lynn
Outfielder	Reggie Jackson
Manager	Gene Mauch

from Long Beach. Center fielder Fred Lynn (.299, 21 HRs, 86 RBIs) was an All-American at USC and a former MVP in Boston. Anaheim-bred left fielder Brian Downing (28 HRs) was as local as they get. So was pitcher Mike Witt, a 6'7" basketball star at Servite High School.

First baseman Rod Carew (.319) was so at home living in Orange County that he may as well have been from there, too. DH Don Baylor contributed 24 homers. Geoff Zahn, a washout with the Dodgers, won 18 games. Ken Forsch added 13 wins.

For all the talent, homegrown or otherwise, it was the acquisition of the great Reggie Jackson that gave this team all their prestige. "Mr. October," already a Hall of Fame player who had propelled the A's and Yankees to five World Championships, was signed to a $900,000-per-year contract for four seasons, with 50 cents for each admission beyond 2.4 million. Season sales escalated from 12,000 to 18,000, and the 2.8 million patrons who came to the Big A made Jackson very wealthy.

That Fred Lynn played at El Monte High School and attended USC, but his football career there was cut short by "one too many hits by Sam 'Bam' Cunningham"? Rod Dedeaux transferred his scholarship to the baseball program. He led the Trojans to the 1971, 1972, and 1973 College World Series championships, twice making All-American. He was disappointed to be drafted behind number-one pick David Clyde in 1973. Lynn became the first player ever to win the Rookie of the Year and MVP awards in the same season, with Boston in 1975.

"From the standpoint of excitement and drawing power, Reggie and Pete Rose are in a class by themselves," Autry proclaimed, adding truthfully that Jackson created an "extra dimension" separating good clubs from championship ones.

Jackson's first act as an Angel was to call Mauch, telling him that any problems he may have had with Billy Martin in New York would not be repeated. Mauch just told him he wanted him to "play for me the way you did against me."

Though 1982 was not Reggie's greatest year in baseball, it was up there. He would hit .275 with 39 home runs and 101 runs batted in. But Jackson's greatest contribution may have been the fact that, despite the great Nolan Ryan, for the very first time the club had a marquee player who helped them overshadow the Dodgers.

The players of that year, many of whom had played for previous teams, were veterans who were hungry to win a title. Proven performers, they were secure in their statistics and place in the game, leading to a team attitude.

Downing saw the team jell. He knew the time was now, stating that they "can't afford to let this opportunity get away."

Oakland was favored at the beginning of the season, but manager Billy Martin wore out his welcome, making ethnic slurs towards the new ownership group while their season slipped away.

California hung in with great hitting and just enough pitching, but it was Bavasi's late-season acquisition of southpaw Tommy John that made the team a real winner. John, a three-time 20-game winner, was long in the tooth, thought to be over the hill. He was not.

His 4–2 record in Anaheim was the difference as the club won the West at 93–69, three games better than Kansas City's 90–72.

Despite their power, "the Little General" (Mauch's nickname) played "little ball" when he needed to, using Foli and Boone to lay down bunts. He rested his regulars just enough so that they did not wear thin down the stretch, which he is not given credit for. It would seem he had learned that lesson from 1964.

The playoffs opened at the Big A, with John mowing down "Harvey's Wallbangers"—a Milwaukee club that swung the bat as well as California in a season dominated by offense. Harvey Kuenn's Brewers featured MVP Robin Yount. John stated that while Cincinnati's Big Red Machine of the 1970s was the best offensive team he had ever faced, he also said the '82 Brewers—as well as the Angels—need not "take a backseat to anyone."

He managed to hold the Brewers in check, 8–3, to the delight of the home crowd. Bruce Kison, a veteran who as a 1971 rookie helped Pittsburgh win the World Series, then responded with a 4–2 Angels win to send the series back to Milwaukee, seemingly in California's hip pocket.

"The Singing Cowboy" was one win from the World Series against his boyhood favorites, St. Louis. Instead of the Fall Classic, however, it was what Ross Newhan called in *The Anaheim Angels: A Complete History*, "A Classic Fall," which he picked up from the *L.A. Times* headline.

Fred Lynn said it was "a tall order" for Milwaukee to beat his team three straight. Reggie Jackson noticed on the team charter to Milwaukee that the club seemed to have "put the cart before the horse."

Milwaukee's Don Sutton stopped them, 5–3, with Paul Molitor hitting a two-run homer off young Mike Witt. Then Mauch rekindled all the Bunning-Short comparisons, sitting scheduled starter Ken Forsch in favor of John, who was not up to the task. The 39-year-old was hit hard in a 9–5 loss. Tied at two games apiece, the Angels had all the momentum taken away, leaving them in the position of being a substantial underdog in the fifth game. Everything seemed to work against them now.

Mauch was testy. John questioned whether his handling of Game 4 had been done the right way. Then Mauch made another debatable move, benching Forsch. He had failed to go more than three innings in his last two regular-season starts. Forsch was sidelined in favor of Kison on short rest with a blood blister on his finger.

Kison managed to hold Milwaukee down, leaving with a 3–2 lead after five innings. The Angels, however, stranded six runners against Pete Vuckovich. They failed to take full advantage of four Brewers errors.

When Mauch failed to bring in southpaw Andy Hassler in the seventh inning to face left-handed swinging Cecil Cooper, who later said Hassler was always "tough on me," Luis Sanchez gave up a two-run single to Cooper with two outs and two strikes against him. It put Milwaukee up 4–3.

Mauch claimed Hassler got his outs on balls and feared a wild pitch. Hassler did come in and was flawless, but he was angry, and it was too late: 4–3 was the final score. The recriminations flew all around, with the consensus being that Mauch had blown it…again.

Bavasi, a former Dodgers executive, said it was worse than the 1951 "shot heard 'round the world" loss to the Giants, because they wanted it so badly for Autry. There would be more disappointments down the road.

Big Don

Texas-born Don Baylor came to the big leagues as a heralded phenom, *The Sporting News'* 1970 Minor League Player of the Year. While he became the 1979 American League Most Valuable Player, and is remembered as one of the all-time favorite Angels, his big-league career did not quite match expectations. This is not an indictment of his career, but rather a testimony to just how much was expected of him.

Baylor was a designated hitter with California and other clubs. DHs are considered less athletic than most of their brethren, yet in Don's case he was a great all-around athlete. The 6'1" Baylor was 195 pounds when he broke in, but looked bigger and stronger than that, especially by the time he played at Anaheim.

Born in Austin, Baylor was a prep football star growing up, but instead of taking his services to Darrell Royal or Chuck Fairbanks, he was selected by Baltimore. The Orioles may have had the best top-to-bottom organization in baseball at the time. They were champions at the big-league level, with great prospects down on the farm. Baylor was immediately installed as the "next Frank Robinson," a lofty moniker to live up to.

Baylor moved up the ladder, slowly but surely. In a lesser organization, he would have reached the majors earlier, but becoming a Baltimore Oriole was no easy task. He tore up minor league pitching each step along the way; a line-drive hitter who developed more power, hitting 22 home runs with 107 RBIs in 140 games at Rochester in 1970. In 1971 frustration began to set in. Called up to play eight games in 1970, the best player in minor league baseball went back to

TRIVIA

**The 1982 Angels featured
four ex-Most Valuable
Players. Who were they?**

Answers to the trivia questions are on pages 189–190.

Rochester, where, to his credit, his production or attitude did not go down, but the big-league call-up did not happen.

In 1972 he broke into the Baltimore lineup after Robinson was traded to Los Angeles. Baylor crowded the plate just like F. Robby, but some questioned whether this tactic, which resulted in his fair share of hit-by-pitches, was not detrimental to his future health.

The team tailed off and Baylor, who hit .253 in 1972, .286 in 1973, and .272 in 1974, took much of the blame. He did not match his minor league power numbers or ultimate expectations. On a team that won with pitching and defense, he was not a defensive stalwart, but he was fast, stealing 24 bases in 1972, 32 in 1973, and 29 in 1974.

Baylor frustrated Baltimore fans. The Orioles could not get past Oakland in the 1973 and 1974 playoffs. Baylor did not knock anybody's socks off in those postseasons.

Just as he was coming into his own, Baylor was traded to Oakland for Reggie Jackson. The A's did not particularly want Baylor, they just wanted to get rid of Jackson before he became a free agent, leaving them with nothing. There was no enthusiasm in Oakland in those sell-off years. A typical Baylor at-bat consisted of popping up with men on to end a rally. The DH would then meander into the A's clubhouse, perhaps emerging within sight of the fans sitting above the clubhouse-to-dugout walkway chomping down on a roast beef sandwich. Fans took to calling him Don "Roast Beef Sandwich" Baylor or Don "Pop-up" Baylor. Fortunately for Baylor, attendance was so low and interest so poor that he probably did not notice.

Further wholesale sell-offs by Charlie O. Finley landed Baylor at Anaheim in 1977. His numbers improved a bit, but nobody was thinking about Frank Robinson anymore when comparing Baylor to anybody. He was not a stiff, but he was one of those talented athletes who seemingly never reach their potential. California's poor showing in 1977 was not blamed on Baylor. He was new and the fans accepted losing as their natural state. Baylor seemed to have been infected more by the "Anaheim syndrome" than he appeared to be a malevolent outside disease, infecting others.

Some athletes just take forever, and *ever* finally occurred in 1978 when Baylor slammed 34 homers and drove in 99. Jim Fregosi, a man's man and former star player—albeit a guy who broke in early and was spectacular almost from the get-go, as opposed to Baylor—impressed the big man known as "Groove" by treating him with respect. He never lied to him, giving him his reasons for doing things. On a winning team, it all made sense.

Despite a career that included the 1979 American League MVP, some thought Don Baylor never quite lived up to expectations. Photo courtesy of Getty Images.

That late-1970s Angels third baseman Carney Lansford led Santa Clara, California, to the 1969 Little League World Series in Williamsport, Pennsylvania?

In 1979 the Angels were a winning team. Baylor carried them on his back, with 36 homers and an astounding 139 RBIs. He also scored 120 runs, indicating others carried him, as well. In Boston, Fred Lynn had an even better year than in his marvelous 1975 rookie season, threatening to capture the Triple Crown. If there was any "East Coast bias" (an overblown concept, really), it did not stop Baylor from garnering the MVP over Lynn and Baltimore's Ken Singleton.

It was in 1979 that Baylor finally lived up to Frank Robinson. No, Baylor is not a Hall of Famer with almost 600 career home runs like Robinson. But he developed leadership qualities based on his past experience with Robinson. Robinson was a clubhouse wit who orchestrated "Kangaroo Courts," which was not really Baylor's style. Rather, the professionalism and work ethic, the desire to win (or the hatred of losing, perhaps even more important) marked Baylor's clubhouse and inspirational contributions to a winning club in need of something to break what many felt was suburban apathy.

In 1980 a wrist injury stopped Baylor just when he was on the verge of stardom; as in all-time-great stardom. The next couple of seasons were frustrating. A strike ruined the game in 1981. Baylor also could not get the Angels to pay him what he felt he was worth. Gene Autry's wife had passed away, and his new wife, Jackie, more or less held the club's purse strings.

Despite hitting 24 homers with 93 RBIs on the division champion Angels of 1982, he was not rewarded for his leadership or performance. Baylor went to New York and had power years at Yankee Stadium. He had a big offensive year playing at Boston in 1986 (31 homers, 94 RBIs) on the team that crushed Angels hearts in the playoffs. In 1988 he toiled for one of the most talented teams ever, the "Bash Brothers" A's, before retiring. He managed in Colorado and with the Chicago Cubs and seems to have beaten back cancer.

All in all, Baylor always maintained his strength and integrity, which he credits to his church upbringing in Texas.

Man of Honor

Rod Carew overcame some of the greatest obstacles imaginable to achieve big-league success. He said what led him away from crime, drugs, alcohol, and depression was baseball. While his tunnel vision for the game no doubt gave him the focus to avoid the many traps set for him, a closer study of the man reveals that, whether he had been a great athlete or not, success would have come his way. That is because Rod Carew is a man of honor. His success might not have been known by millions of sports fans, but it would have been known by his family, his friends, and by God, which is even more important.

It started out as inauspiciously as possible. In an oft-told story, Carew's mother was pregnant and traveling by train in Panama. She went into labor. A doctor on the train, Rodney Cline, delivered the infant. Mrs. Carew was so grateful she named the boy Rodney Cline Carew.

But growing up in the Canal Zone in a poor, but not impoverished family, Carew withstood regular beatings from his father, Erick. Sometimes drunk, usually violent, Erick beat up Rodney and his mother. It was the desire to escape and play baseball that led Carew away from trouble, which at one point meant contemplating taking a machete to his sleeping father. Carew realized that if he did that, his father would be dead, he would be in jail, his mother would have nothing, and his soul would be in grave danger. He continued to endure.

He listened to the Armed Forces Radio Network, which carried big-league baseball, and knew everything about the American stars. Latin American players like Roberto Clemente, Camilo Pascual, and Luis Aparicio were breaking into the game, giving him hope.

Rod Carew at spring training on April 2, 1982.

But his big "break" occurred when his mother finally had enough of Erick Carew, moving to New York City with Rodney and his siblings. Incredibly, the intelligent Carew learned English, but not broken English. He sounds like a college professor.

New York was like a playground for the young baseball star, who played on a sandlot within the shadows of Yankee Stadium. Already a huge fan from his years listening to the Armed Forces baseball broadcasts, he soaked up the atmosphere. But it took a few years, as he had to work to help support his mother. In his senior year of high school, though, he starred on a city league team and was given a try-out by the Minnesota Twins when they visited Yankee Stadium.

When Carew started spraying line drives all over the famous arena, Twins manager Sam Mele said, "Get him out of here! I don't want the Yankees seeing him." He was assigned to the Twins' minor league system. Three years later, he was the American League Rookie of the Year. In 1969 he led the league with a .332 average. In 1970 he would have erased any batting title aspirations of Alex

Johnson or Carl Yastrzemski but was hurt after 51 games with a .366 average.

From 1972 to 1975 he captured four straight batting titles and through 1978 earned six in seven years. He had more than 200 hits four times, and in 1977 was the American League Most Valuable Player when he pounded 239 hits and came within a few "seeing eyes" of .400 (.388).

As a free agent Carew was romanced by the Yankees, his (sort of) hometown team. But Carew liked California. He liked the neighborhood around Anaheim Stadium. His ordered mind told him to become an Angel, not subjecting himself to the "Bronx Zoo."

Carew batted .318 (1979), .331 (1980), .305 (1981), .319 (1982), .339 (1983), .295 (1984), and .280 (1985). He finished with 3,053 hits and was elected on his first ballot to the Hall of Fame.

Aside from his great batting skills, Carew possessed uncommon speed and base-stealing ability. He certainly legged out his share of infield singles and drag bunt hits, helping his batting average. In 1969, playing under daredevil manager Billy Martin at Minnesota, Carew tied Ty Cobb's American League record with six steals of home.

Carew was part of a new generation of American Leaguers who played aggressive offensive baseball. The National League, first to bring in a large influx of black players, had taken the lead in this area. They played what came to be known as "National League baseball." The Yankees were the only team that had the ability to sit back and wait for the long ball. When they fell in the late 1960s, the senior circuit was decidedly better. Carew, Mickey Rivers, Tommy Harper, and then the fast, aggressive Athletics changed the balance of power back to the Americans.

Carew also "owed" much of his success to Nolan Ryan. When Ryan first came to the American League, his high heat was too much even for Carew. In order to "catch up" with Ryan's fastball, Carew changed his stance, bending his knees and giving

TRIVIA

On August 4, 1985, the day Rod Carew collected his 3,000th career hit, which other superstar attained a baseball milestone?

Answers to the trivia questions are on pages 189–190.

DID YOU KNOW . . . That Rod Carew also played for Angels managers Bill Rigney (1970) and Gene Mauch (1976–78) at Minnesota?

himself a split second head start on the "Ryan Express." He certainly never "owned" Ryan, but he was no longer owned *by* him.

Carew's adjustments with Ryan on the mound led to similar tinkering with his stance depending upon which other pitchers he faced. In the dead-ball era, Ty Cobb and other stars of the period described themselves as "scientific" hitters. The influence of Babe Ruth and the power hitters who followed decreased the scientific approach. Carew revolutionized the game, figuring out a way to become wealthy as a singles hitter.

Pitchers never could find a pattern with Carew. He was very smart, knew himself, and knew each pitcher in the league. He often could "call" a pitch as it was leaving the pitcher's hand. Many thought he was stealing signs, but he just figured out tendencies.

Carew was shy by nature, probably the result of his battered childhood. In 1977, when he flirted with .400, he could not avoid getting major attention from the press. Ted Williams, the last to achieve that figure, was a big fan of Carew's.

"A picture-book athlete," he told *Sports Illustrated*. "His swing is a thing of beauty. So smooth, he seems to be doing everything without trying."

Carew made the cover of *Time* magazine; he was a long way from the Canal Zone. After winning another batting title in 1978, Carew was traded to California because the Twins knew they would not be able to meet his free-agent contract demands at season's end. His free-agent negotiations effectively took place in 1979, a year early. Buzzy Bavasi paid him $4.4 million to play for the Angels.

Carew's decision to play in California instead of New York paid off when the Yankees faltered in 1979, while the Angels won the division. Had he been in New York in 1980 and 1981, however, he might have been the extra ingredient they needed to go all the way in years in which the Bronx Bombers made the postseason but did not win.

Carew was a devoted family man. Ultimately, his decision came down to the clean streets of Orange County over the mean streets of New York City. After joining the Angels, *The Sporting News* featured him. Carew, it turned out, was a "neat freak," a man of consummate good habits and order. He told *The Sporting News* writer that he washed, gassed, and checked the oil in his car every day. His routines—what time he got up, what he ate, what he wore, how he prepared for the game—were as planned as a military campaign.

Carew's family meant everything to him, which made it so sad when his daughter Michelle passed away from cancer in 1996. Carew, a private man, did not want publicity, but he realized that his daughter's plight could generate attention and money for leukemia research. His upstanding reputation over 30 years in baseball helped generate needed funds, as well as increased awareness of the risks endemic to African Americans and people of color. Always a religious man, Carew prayed for Michelle just as he had prayed for himself when his father battered him. It was faith that allowed him to deal with the irony—a man treated poorly by his father, who loved his own daughter with everything he had, only to have her taken away.

Carew was an Angels batting coach for a number of years, considered one of the better teachers in the game. Just as he had been when he played, Carew was an innovator, always thinking outside the box.

Reggie! Reggie!

In many ways, Reginald Martinez Jackson represents the dividing line between baseball's old ways and its new. He is partly Hispanic, partly black, and entirely of the so-called "New Breed" of minority athletes populating sports in the 1960s.

In his great book, *October 1964*, David Halberstam painted a portrait of the 1964 Cardinals-Yankees World Series from a sociopolitical point of view. After Jackie Robinson broke the color line, black athletes were of a certain "type." Generally this meant that they were intelligent without being "clubhouse lawyers." Family men, not carousers. Christian. Team players. Quiet.

Football star Jim Brown broke from that mold, and the '64 Cardinals had their share of educated, proud, high-strung black guys with attitude: Bob Gibson, Curt Flood, Bill White. This kind of black ballplayer realized that as long as he produced on the field, he had leeway that the rest of society did not accord the black population. But as Flood later discovered, the boundaries only went so far.

During the 11-year period (1965–1976) in which the Yankees were "exiled" to the baseball version of Elba, two teams—the Baltimore Orioles and the Oakland A's—emerged as the two main American League contenders. Oakland got the upper hand, winning three straight World Championships from 1972 to 1974.

The "head of the ticket" on those teams was Reggie Jackson. He was, as mentioned, of the New Breed—outspoken, articulate, proud. But the other dividing line he straddled was of the economic variety. Jackson was not the first free agent, but Jackson's signing with the Yankees before the 1977 season had the greatest impact. He was of that class of athlete who made enough money that he

Reggie Jackson comes out of the dugout to the applause of the crowd at New York's Yankee Stadium after his 23rd home run of the season in the eighth inning of a game against the Yankees on July 24, 1982.

TOP 10

All-Time Home-Run List as of the Start of the 2006 Season

Player	Home Runs
1. Hank Aaron	755
2. Barry Bonds	734
3. Babe Ruth	714
4. Willie Mays	660
5. Sammy Sosa	588
6. Frank Robinson	586
7. Mark McGwire	583
8. Harmon Killebrew	573
9. Rafael Palmeiro	569
10. Reggie Jackson	563

could practically call his own shots, rising above the politics of traditional owner-player and manager-player relationships. Fireworks came of this paradigm shift. Verbal battles, chess matches, and sometimes even physical altercations between Jackson and his two principal owners, Charlie O. Finley and later George Steinbrenner, and with Yankees manager Billy Martin. It all made for headlines, merging the blurry line between sports and entertainment.

Jackson was pure entertainment. In the "steroid era," his records pale somewhat, but based on what we now know about Barry Bonds, Mark McGwire, Sammy Sosa, and many others, Jackson and players such as Willie Mays, Hank Aaron, Babe Ruth, Ted Williams, Mickey Mantle, Ken Griffey Jr., and Frank Thomas, just to name a few, can reclaim much of their "lost" stature.

Jackson was the essence of a winner, which is not the same as a team player. But when it comes to rings and putting money in his teammates' pockets, it is the highest of accolades. "Mr. October" was a clutch hitter in big games like no player before or since, and with all due respect this includes stalwarts like Ruth, Mantle, and...the list is that short!

When it comes to being a "money player," Aaron, Mays, Bonds, and Williams are not in his league. A handful of pitchers, like Christy Mathewson, Whitey Ford, Sandy Koufax, Bob Gibson, and Oakland teammate Jim "Catfish" Hunter, were to their positions what Reggie was to his. Perhaps Michael Jordan and Jerry West in basketball, Joe Montana and Johnny Unitas in football are in this pantheon. Perhaps.

Reggie grew up in a broken home that split his youth between middle-class Philadelphia, where his father was a successful businessman, and the Baltimore projects. Reggie starred in baseball and football. His Adonis physique was natural, not just from the absence of steroids but mainly without the use of weights, at least by modern training standards. He went to Arizona State University, where he played for two legends: the grandfatherly Bobby Winkles in baseball and the disciplinarian Frank Kush in football.

In the summers he played for Mama Leone's, a storied Baltimore semi-pro baseball team that was once featured in *Sports Illustrated*. Winkles called the Mama Leone's coach and told him about Reggie. Reggie called the man and arranged a meeting. When the coach saw Jackson, his mouth dropped. He could not previously conceive that a man of color could be so polite and articulate. Jackson learned that his athletic skills combined with intelligence gave him power few minorities possessed. He has made full use of this power in all the years since.

At Arizona State, Reggie played on the 1965 ASU freshman team. The varsity won the national championship. In 1966 Reggie was an All-American and *The Sporting News* Player of the Year. The ASU program formed the basis of the A's champions. Jackson, Rick Monday, and Sal Bando played at ASU and in Oakland. Even Winkles would one day be an Oakland (and Angels) manager.

Jackson was the second player chosen in the 1966 free-agent draft. He was sent to Birmingham, Alabama, ground zero of the 1960s civil rights struggle. Charlie O. Finley was originally from Birmingham. The story varies. One says that one night he was in town entertaining Alabama football coach Paul "Bear" Bryant at a Birmingham game.

The other version is that Bear was at a game because his son, Paul Jr., was the club's general manager. Whether Finley was with

Bryant and invited him into the A's clubhouse, whether Bryant came into the clubhouse at the invitation of his son, or whether the scene played itself out several times, what Bear saw there was the shirtless, muscled Jackson, who he was introduced to. Bryant took one look at the former Sun Devils football star with the intelligent smile. Jackson quietly shook his hand and said that he had "heard a lot about you."

According to Jackson: "Bryant smiled, looked away from me over to his son, and said very matter-of-factly, 'Now this is the kind of nigger boy I need to start my football program.'"

Jackson, to his credit, understood the context of the meeting. "I knew he didn't mean any harm with those words," wrote Jackson in his autobiography, *Reggie* (1984). "This was the best he could do, his way of paying me a compliment. He was drawing on his own experience, his own life, and trying to be nice."

"Yessir," added Bear, "if I could just have one like you, I could get it done real easy at school."

There are many who dispute Bryant's use of the term *nigger*. This author, in researching my book *September 1970: One Night, Two Teams, and the Game That Changed a Nation* (the story of the 1970 USC-Alabama game, which effectively helped end segregation in the South), spoke with many blacks who played or coached for him over a 13-year period. All of them insist he never talked like that. Perhaps he said *nigra*, and Reggie misunderstood. Either way, it foretold unfolding events. Four years later, after Southern California thumped Alabama at Legion Field, Bryant integrated his program. Later evidence uncovered the fact that he and USC coach John McKay had been planning the best way to effectuate this change going back to before or right around his meeting with Jackson.

After hitting 47 home runs in 1969, Jackson warred with the miserly Finley over his contract. The animosity was hot and heavy throughout his disappointing 1970 season. In Chicago, Jackson had to be restrained from going after the owner in the stands during a game.

By 1971 a truce was in place. With it came Oakland glory. Jackson powered 32 home runs to lead the A's to the division title. In an era dominated by pitching, Jackson's stats were not Bonds-like, but his winning records were superior. He hit 25 homers in 1972 to

DID YOU KNOW . . . That Reggie Jackson went to Arizona State to play football, but tried out for the baseball team to win a bet, and also to avoid coach Frank Kush's rigorous spring football practices? After hitting several balls 430 feet over the center-field fence at Sun Devil Field, Reggie asked coach Bobby Winkles if he had made the team, to which Winkles replied, "I think we could find a place for you."

lead Oakland to the American League title. Baltimore finally gave way to the newcomers from the West Coast.

In the playoffs, Jackson's clutch steal of home on a first-and-third situational play barely gave the A's the fifth game, a 2–1 win over Detroit, but cost the team their best player for the World Series with Cincinnati. Jackson badly tore his hamstring and had to watch the Series in street clothes on crutches.

In one of the greatest examples of good pitching beating good hitting this side of Sandy Koufax and Don Drysdale, Oakland prevailed in seven games. The next year, Jackson was the league MVP, carrying the team on his shoulders over Baltimore and then the Tom Seaver–Jon Matlack–Jerry Koosman Mets in the Series.

"You'd sit down with Charlie," he once said, "and he'd say, 'Why, this man hit 15 fewer home runs than he had in this previous season,' or 'Why should I pay a man more to hit seven fewer homers?' or 'He drove in 118 runs in 1969 and only 118 [actually 117] in 1973. Why, that's not improvement!' I'd walk out of those meetings just saying, 'Why, I must be horseshit!'"

Jackson's financial squabbles with Finley never ended. In 1976 he was traded to Baltimore. In 1977 he signed a huge free-agent contract with the Yankees, entering the carnival atmosphere of New York just as the Yankees were emerging from an 11-year (by Yankee standards) slump. His three homers in Game 6, and five overall, powered New York over the Dodgers in the 1977 World Series. He led New York again over Los Angeles in 1978. In 1982 he starred on the California Angels' West Division champions.

Jackson seemed particularly comfortable with the Angels. Always known as a "man about town," he took to the Newport Beach lifestyle of hot clubs and hotter girls. Throughout his career, Jackson was spotted with astonishingly beautiful women in restaurants and public settings, almost as if advertising his prowess for all to see.

In Oakland, he lived in the Berkeley hills, and has maintained his residence there, in Monterey, and in New York, where he has been kept on retainer as a Yankees coach, advisor, and consultant for years.

But the Orange County experience suited him. He played on fabulous teams in Oakland, but attendance was down. It was not a big enough stage to satisfy his giant ego. He took a huge bite out of the

TRIVIA

Reggie Jackson enjoyed playing in California, where he attracted less media attention. What first got him in trouble in New York?

Answers to the trivia questions are on pages 189–190.

Big Apple, perhaps more than he could ultimately swallow. He made a bid to attain that special kind of *gravitas* reserved by society only for the most larger-than-life New York sports icon. In the end, perhaps with some argument, New York would accept Reggie in the elite club whose small membership includes Babe Ruth, Lou Gehrig, Joe DiMaggio, Mickey Mantle, Derek Jeter, Frank Gifford, Joe Namath, and Tom Seaver. The absence of many obvious names from this list only emphasizes how exclusive it is.

But Reggie's years in New York were tumultuous. The kind of press adoration eventually reserved for Mantle and even Seaver was replaced by a "gotcha" mentality in the post-Watergate period. By the time he arrived in Anaheim, he was worn down by the pressure. If a public man like Jackson could be worn down by such a thing, any player could be. He was grateful to play in the friendly confines of the Big A; to be paid his worth by an admiring owner; and to deal with a fair press corps. In true Reggie style, he elevated the Angels to the national stage in a manner they had never known before.

Reggie hit over 500 homers and earned five rings. In 1973 and 1977, in particular, he came through on the biggest of all stages in the most spectacular of manners. He is a Hall of Famer and true legend whose personality and ego matches his talent.

Jackson has straddled the historical line between being an Oakland Athletic and a Yankee, both of whom claim him jealously,

Curses

Pick up the *Baseball Encyclopedia*, or some other diamond reference book. Check out the 1986 California Angels. You will not see nearly the statistical star power, the offensive greatness of the 1979 or 1982 division champions. What you will see is a veteran team, in some cases over the hill. You will not see Rod Carew, let go to make way for Wally Joyner. You will not see Don Baylor, long gone by then. You will see Reggie Jackson, but you will not see Reggie Jackson numbers.

You will see veterans hanging on. There was Brian Downing with 20 homers and 95 RBIs; not bad, but not up to his old standards. You will see Doug DeCinces driving in 96 runs but only hitting .256. You will see Bob Boone at .222.

You will see Bobby Grich, George Hendrick, and the retread Rick Burleson; none of them contributing much. You will see forgettable names like Rob Wilfong, Dick Schofield, Ruppert Jones, and Garry Pettis.

Offensively, to quote Gertrude Stein, there was not much "there there."

The pitching staff? Some promising youth, perhaps. Mike Witt won 18 with a 2.84 ERA, but his potential was never realized over the years. Kirk McCaskill (17–10) was little more than a one-shot wonder.

Don Sutton, of course, was old in 1986 but still a winner (15–11)—although he somehow managed to give up two home runs to Buddy Biancalana of Kansas City one afternoon at the Big A, a feat unto itself. The rest? John Candelaria, Ron Romanick, Doug Corbett, Jim Slaton, an aging Terry Forster...the 1954 Indians they were not.

Then, of course, there was closer Donnie Moore. Some quality in a sea of mediocrity. He had promise to go along with his 21 saves and 2.97 ERA. Also, a sore arm at the end. Read on.

Yet this is remembered as the team that got closest—until 2002—to the brass ring. True, the West was less won than handed over. All it took was to do better than Texas with their 87 victories. In winning 92 with the cast of misfits, kids, and Methuselahs at his disposal, Gene Mauch did his best managing in this star-crossed campaign.

It started in an exciting manner when Wally Joyner lit up Palm Springs. After making the lineup, he started out strong and had fans talking about "Wally World," a reference to the Disney-esque destination of the unfortunate Griswold family in *National Lampoon's Vacation*.

Joyner was their genuine star: .290, 22 home runs, 100 runs batted in, with classic left-handed glove work at first base. The fresh-faced Mormon kid from Georgia was seemingly born for Orange County, and he had a good enough career, but like much of the spirit of '86, his future, like many of his teammates, did not match expectations.

Joyner's early success helped divert attention from the dismissal of Carew and the handling of Jackson. New general manager Mike Port was perceived as cold, but he was carrying out the wishes of Autry. Most say that by then second wife Jackie was calling the shots, not Gene.

Jackie Autry supposedly told Jackson he should retire. The point was debated by the Autrys, who may have talked of the best time for athletes to retire without specifically suggesting they meant for Reggie to ride off into the sunset just yet. Jackson loved Newport Beach, but as much as he enjoyed the lifestyle, he knew it was a business and still felt he could contribute.

The year 1986 saw the third in a string of milestones over the past years. Jackson had reached 500 career homers in 1984. Rod Carew had gotten his 3,000th hit in 1985. On June 18, the 41-year-old Sutton got victory number 300. There is some irony, however, in that all three of these Angels did their best work for many long years in other uniforms prior to arriving in Anaheim.

TOP 10

Worst "Dives" in Baseball History

	Year	Team	Loss
1.	1951	Brooklyn Dodgers	14 games up in August, lose to Giants
2.	1964	Philadelphia Phillies	Mauch's team loses 10 straight to blow pennant
3.	1969	Chicago Cubs	complete September collapse to "Amazin' Mets"
4.	1986	California Angels	Hendu's homer and 3–1 series lead lost
5.	2004	New York Yankees	only team to ever blow 3–0 playoff lead
6.	1984	Chicago Cubs	2–0 series lead, total collapse to Padres
7.	1995	California Angels	fastest 10½-game lead ever blown
8.	1978	Boston Red Sox	14 up over New York on July 17, lose playoff to Yanks
9.	1982	California Angels	up two in best-of-five, Brewers come back
10.	2003	Chicago Cubs	Bartman's grab followed by classic fold

The American League West was a battle until August, when California took the lead to stay over Texas, opened up a 10-game advantage, and coasted in with five to spare.

"Until we win it," said Downing, "none of us can ever forget Milwaukee."

They would "forget" Milwaukee, all right, but not for the reasons Downing had in mind. Waiting for them were...drum roll, please...the Boston Red Sox!

The name alone connotes weirdness and disaster, and in October 1986 weirdness and disaster hung in the air like something

> **DID YOU KNOW . . .** That Gene Mauch's sister married Roy Smalley Jr., a Pacific Coast League All-Star, longtime major leaguer, and friend of Mauch's? Their son, Roy Smalley III, was an All-American on national championship teams at USC and an All-Star shortstop for Mauch's Minnesota Twins in the 1970s.

Shakespeare wrote about in *Macbeth*, a play rife with witches, potent brews, and prophetic warnings of ill tidings to come.

The Angels and the Red Sox? Oh, man! Talk about a riddle, surrounded by a puzzle, wrapped inside an enigma...

These were the two most star-crossed teams in baseball here.

The "Curse of the Bambino" began when Red Sox owner Harry Frazee sold Babe Ruth to the Yankees in 1920.

The "Angels Curse" started when they moved from L.A. to Orange County in 1966, losing their character in suburbia. Just a few of the disasters to befall the franchise prior to 1986 include:

- Relief ace Minnie Rojas being paralyzed in a car accident in 1970.
- Chico Ruiz threatening Alex Johnson with a gun in the clubhouse in 1971.
- Mike Miley, an Angel from 1975 to 1976, dying in a car accident.
- Lyman Bostock signing an enormous free-agent contract in 1978, just before being shot dead by a jealous husband.

The team's mascot should have been a black cat.

Then there was Boston. "The war to end all wars" in 1918 was still a more recent development than any World Series victory won by the Bosox as of 1986.

So when these guys got together in the '86 playoffs, it was bad karma. The witching hour. You could just feel it, something had to go terribly wrong. What did you expect out of a club managed by Gene Mauch? They called him "the Little General," and like Napoleon he had already experienced his personal Waterloo in 1964, when he pitched Philadelphia's Jim Bunning and Chris Short on short rest during a 10-game losing streak, allowing St. Louis to win the pennant.

He had been exiled to Elba (Montreal, actually), but now the Fremont High infielder was at home, tanned and relaxed, a new man.

Still, when California won the West and Boston cruised the East, led by "Rocket Roger" Clemens, who won his first 14 decisions en route to a 24-victory season that would earn him A.L. MVP and Cy Young honors, hope sprang eternal. The teams split the first two at Fenway, and California won Game 3.

In Game 4 on Saturday night, Boston manager John McNamara went to the Mauch playbook, pitching Clemens on short rest. Rocket lost it just in time, blowing a 3–0 ninth inning lead, as the Angels won in the eleventh, 4–3. This was the beginning of the "Clemens Curse," which he would not end until he switched to Yankees pinstripes in 1999.

Neither team seemed even slightly willing to win on Sunday afternoon at the Big A.

Red Sox outfielder Dave Henderson looked like Charlie Chaplin in *Modern Times*, stumbling and confused while an innocent pop-up dropped in for a double, then letting a Bobby Grich drive bounce out of his mitt and over the fence for a homer, giving California the lead.

Ahead 5–2, champagne was brought into the Angels clubhouse in the ninth.

Don Baylor's two-run homer made it 5–4.

Boston relief pitcher Joe Sambito said, "Wait" to the security guards who were beginning to pack the bullpen equipment.

Mike Witt got Dwight Evans for the second out. Gary Lucas came in to pitch to Rich Gedman, who asked that a center-field banner—Another Boston Choke—be removed. Lucas hit Gedman.

Mauch brought the right-handed Donnie Moore in to face the right-handed "Hendu."

Moore had that "deer in the headlights" look working to Henderson. He got two strikes on him, just for some drama, before sticking a "nothing" forkball in his wheelhouse. Henderson's homer made it 6–5, Boston.

Hey, forget this part? California tied it in the bottom of the ninth, but Moore hit Baylor leading off the eleventh, and he scored. Calvin

Schiraldi, another choke artist, got some redemption by stopping the Angels. The big crowd went home in stunned silence.

The Angels reacted to adversity like the French Army in 1940, losing at Fenway 10–4 and 8–1, sending Boston to the fall classic.

Then the Red Sox became the second team to blow a Series after winning the first two on the road against the 108-win Mets. Of course, it had to happen, and to a New York team at that. Boston blew Game 6 when Bill Buckner let Mookie Wilson's 100-hopper go under his legs. Schiraldi looked like he wanted to be anywhere but on the Shea Stadium mound.

Hey, it was fate. Donnie Moore? The worst fate of them all. On July 18, 1989, a few miles from Anaheim Stadium, his promising career having nosedived since the Henderson homer, Moore shot his wife, then, with his kids watching, shot himself dead.

Casualties? Moore, McNamara, Buckner, Schiraldi, Clemens, Mauch, et al.

As Jim Morrison once said, "No one here gets out alive."

Abbott Remains
Inspiration to Millions

This author had a good friend at USC who was supposedly "handi-capped" by the use of only one arm. However, this guy was a good student, active in athletics, probably the best driver I ever saw—a guy with an uncanny knack for finding a good parking space any-where. I am talking about the Rainbow on Sunset Boulevard on a Saturday night. If I drove I would have to park three miles away. This guy provided curb service! He loved sports and became involved in his son's Little League activities in Connecticut. My friend contacted me when I was a columnist for *StreetZebra* and told me I should write a story about somebody who was an inspiration to him—former California Angels' pitcher Jim Abbott.

"He was a phenom in many respects," my friend, Bob Karl, said of him. "I think the bottom line is that being without a hand is like not being handicapped at all in that exceptional coordination com-pensates for it. For example, I have been playing football, baseball, billiards, tennis, table tennis, basketball, among many other sports, and defeat the majority of my peers. I just feel that Abbott had awesome accomplishments. He did get an opportunity to hit and came through with some big ones during the 1999 season. One other note is he was out of baseball for the entire '97 season and worked his way back from single A ball in '98, struggling at each minor league level, and won his last five starts. Quite a comeback indeed. Might want to add that Jim Abbott, who I have met, is a class act and never snubs fans as a Pete Rose would do."

Abbott is an inspiration not just to Bob Karl, but for millions.

He was "handicapped" by the use of one arm, but oh, what an arm it was. He was one of the greatest college baseball pitchers of all

125

time at the University of Michigan, where he was 26–8 with a 3.03 ERA from 1986 to 1989. After being drafted in 1985, he was an All-American for the Wolverines, won the Golden Spikes award, and came to national attention by beating the vaunted Cubans. He pitched in the '88 Olympics in Seoul, South Korea. In 1988 the Angels made him their first draft pick. Without pitching a day in the minor leagues, Abbott became an Angels starter, going an impressive 12–12 in his rookie year. He was named to the Topps All-Rookie team, and was only the 15th player in baseball history to go straight to the big

TRIVIA

Aside from Jim Abbott, what other left-handed pitcher might be considered the best baseball player ever produced by the University of Michigan?

Answers to the trivia questions are on pages 189–190.

leagues without playing in the minors. In 1991 he was 18–11 with a 2.89 ERA, striking out 158 to 73 walks in 243 innings. He finished third that season in the Cy Young voting. Abbott was never on the disabled list until 1992, and then for sprained ribs.

Abbott was a Yankee for two years, 1993 and 1994, threw a no-hitter against Cleveland at Yankee Stadium, and in 1995 returned to Anaheim from Chicago. He won 11 on the year. His performance slipped considerably in 1996 when he suffered a 2–18 season with a 7.48 ERA at Anaheim, but his support that season was horrendous. The fact is, a pitcher has to be pretty good to lose 18 games.

Abbott posted a 6.91 ERA at Milwaukee in 1999, and by 2000 his remarkable career had run its course. But hey, he had a great run and every reason to be proud. His "handicap" ceased being a story years ago because it was not a handicap, and that was his greatest contribution. What may have been his most impressive trait was the fact that he was a flawless fielder who once handled 46 straight chances without an error. He perfected the transfer of glove from under his arm to his hand, would remove the ball, lose the glove, and make the throw. He was awesome.

Abbott was a fan favorite everywhere he played, but it had nothing to do with being humbled by his one-armed status. The fact is, he could have played the sympathy card, the victim looking for

California Angels pitcher Jim Abbott delivers against the New York Yankees on May 27, 1996, in Anaheim.

That aside from Jim Abbott, other disabled
players included Dummy Hoy, a mute outfielder for eight
different teams from 1888 to 1902; and Pete Gray, a one-armed
World War II outfielder for the St. Louis Browns? In addition, pitcher Bert
Shephard returned to the Senators after losing a leg in World War II. Monte
Stratton of the White Sox (Jimmy Stewart depicted him in the movie) played
in the minors with a wooden leg after a hunting accident. A movie about
Abbott is begging to be produced!

special favors. He could have bragged about how great he was, and
not just "great for being a one-armed pitcher." Abbott was the Big
Man on Campus at Michigan, where star athletes are treated like
demigods. His accomplishments are not seen in the light of his disability. He is simply judged on the merits as any other pitcher is
judged. In this regard he holds up with contemporaries Chuck Finley
and Mark Langston. When they were all in their prime the Angels
could make a legitimate argument that they had the three best starting southpaw pitchers ever.

There is no evidence that Abbott's career was any less because of
his condition. It does not seem that he got tired, mentally or physically, dealing with it, or that injury resulted from it. Perhaps he could
have lasted longer and been greater. His ability seemed to be
Cooperstown-esque, but the same thing could be said of Finley and
Langston.

Abbott just went about producing excellence. The truth of his
excellence poured forth like water irrigating a barren valley. It was
not the kind of truth he needed to shout about. One saw it and therefore knew it. That is the best kind.

"The Grandest Gentleman in the Game"

In *The Glory of Their Times*, former A's pitcher Rube Bressler told Lawrence Ritter that Hall of Famer Chief Bender was "one of the finest and kindest men who ever lived." It would seem that people do not talk like that anymore, except that sometimes they do.

They do when they are high-quality people talking about other high-quality people. So it was when Jim Abbott described Jimmie Reese, the most beloved Angel of them all. For 23 years Reese was a fixture with a fungo bat. For true fans who enjoy getting out to the ballpark early to watch batting practice, pitchers running wind sprints, and infielders honing their craft handling between-the-BP-pitch grounders, Reese was a maestro.

The art of hitting grounders to infielders, especially when batting practice is going on, is just that: an art. It is one of those things that looks easy. Average fans, even good athletes from other sports, even good *baseball players*, are not equipped to hit practice grounders.

The ball must be hit swiftly, skimming along the ground, not a rocket shot and not a slow dribbler. It must be hit within range of the fielder. It is not "go to your left" or "go to your right" practice; rather, it is the repetition of hand-eye coordination, of seeing the bounding ball smoothly into the glove on a consistent basis. The poor infield-ground-ball hitter quickly learns how easy it is to miss the ball, barely tip the ball, pop it up, hit line drives, or other embarrassments that quickly earn total scorn from the waiting fielder, as well as all other observers.

Reese was the master, handling the twirling bat as if it were an extension of his body; the hitting of it, the shifting of the bat to the

---

TRIVIA

At one time Jimmie Reese roomed with Babe Ruth. What other famous baseball personality roomed with the Babe, but with near-disastrous results?

Answers to the trivia questions are on pages 189–190.

other hand, the handling of the ball usually on a bounce from the fielder or tossed from a cut-off man. Then, of course, the transfer of ball to air, free hand to bat—an action not unlike Abbott's shifting of glove from under-arm to hand—and the clean striking of the ball at precisely the right angle. All of this must be done within the window of a few seconds in between the batting practice pitch and subsequent hit. To mix it up is to threaten the fielder's health with the prospect of a "screaming meemie" from the hitter while he is concentrating on the practice grounder.

Finally, the artist must work in a confined space, careful to avoid hitting one of the many bystanders—reporters, cameramen, milling hitters, coaches—with his flailing fungo bat.

Reese also was the best at another key coaching duty: smoothing egos. Jimmie Reese joined the Angels at the age of 70. Perhaps he was not managerial material, that job requiring the need to kick some butt, to yell and motivate, to argue with umpires and tell players they are being shipped to the minors, to Kansas City, or oblivion.

But Reese was simply everybody's favorite. He was a gentle soul in a baseball uniform. Women and less-knowledgeable fans would wonder at the kindly looking fellow surrounded by all that *machismo*.

Reese had seen it all. His roommate was once Babe Ruth.

"I never actually saw Babe," Reese said. "I roomed with his suitcase."

That, of course, was a joke made by other roommates of party hounds, notably Albie Pearson describing his relationship with Bo Belinsky.

Reese reached the major leagues but was better known for his 12 years in the Pacific Coast League. When the PCL voted its all-time all-star team, Reese was the second baseman.

Reese came to Anaheim in 1972. Until that time, the club was known first for its Sunset Strip antics, then for the volatile Chico Ruiz–Alex Johnson gun incident. Reese's kindly demeanor seemed just the ticket. Manager Bobby Winkles, like Reese a fatherly sort

Jimmie Reese was widely loved and admired by players, coaches, management, and fans. Photo courtesy of Getty Images.

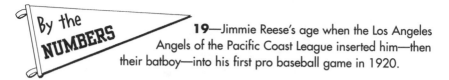

19—Jimmie Reese's age when the Los Angeles Angels of the Pacific Coast League inserted him—then their batboy—into his first pro baseball game in 1920.

who came from the collegiate ranks, did not have the fire for big-league managing and was eventually let go.

But Reese was kept on because amid all the swearing and blasphemy, human compassion always has its place. While Tom Morgan is credited with tightening Nolan Ryan's pitching motion, giving him the tools to harness that overwhelming fastball, it was Reese who helped Ryan the most.

Reese recognized that Ryan was not in shape. He worked him until he had the legs of a big-league starter.

Reese helped Ryan make the transition from New York to Anaheim, from prospect to star, at a time when the pitcher was a young husband and father, unsure of whether he was doing right by his family. While the other players scattered to bars and broads, Ryan drove to Anaheim to see wife Ruth every night during the 1972 spring training.

It was Reese who Ryan confided to, spent time with, poured out his country insecurities to. He loved the old man so much that he named his second son Nolan Reese Ryan. By that time, Nolan was a *bona fide* star, and in his mind he owed much to Jimmie. The two were inseparable. When Ryan departed, Reese took it hard.

"It broke me up; it broke my heart," said Reese. "I didn't think they could do it. I didn't think there was a chance in the world the Angels would let him get away. That anyone would let him get away. That anyone anywhere would ever let him get away."

"To me, he was the consummate patriarch of baseball," said Bobby Grich, who took so many of those well-placed Reese fungos.

When a player contributed to the cause, Reese would slowly walk over to him, put his hand on his knee, and say, "Atta boy."

"It felt like the icing on the cake," said Grich.

So beloved was Reese that he was one of only six Angels to have their uniform numbers retired by the club. In 1994 he passed away at the age of 92.

Wally World

Wally Joyner is not the greatest of all Angels; not by a long shot. Furthermore, his great association with the team was cut drastically short by his leaving them too soon for Kansas City, where he labored in obscurity on mediocre clubs.

Joyner is like Jim Abbott, in that he made a spectacular debut, appeared to be somebody who would establish a national following, but did not. He is a product of the 1986 season: a disappointing year, in which the players on that team and on the following Angels teams—Mark Langston, Chuck Finley—did not live up to hopes and dreams.

However, with the value of some 21 years hindsight, 1986 seems innocent by today's standards. Joyner was almost that last vestige of innocence. He was young, fresh-faced, and talented. My, he was talented. The hopes attached to him as he was making his mark at Palm Springs in March of 1986 seem to be the kind of hopes that no longer resonate.

Joyner appeared to be an Angel for the next 20 years. The fact that he did not leads the modern cynic to look at all of the current Wally Joyners, concluding that great rookies are there for a few years—until free agency, arbitration, and agents come along to effect further damage to our national pastime.

Anaheim Stadium was renamed "Wally World" in his honor. He was elected a starter for the 1986 All-Star Game by *write-in vote*. The player he beat out? Don Mattingly, a superstar who was on the ballot and had all the New York fan base in his favor. Joyner made fans forget a Hall of Famer, Rod Carew. Through July 1986 he was hitting

.315 with 21 homers. He provided power at a power position that Carew did not.

A mid-July injury brought his numbers down. From August 1 on, he hit .235 with one home run. The Angels won the division, though Joyner lost out on the Rookie of the Year vote to Jose Canseco. He was 5-for-11 in three games in the disaster with Boston but had to be hospitalized with a staph infection in his injured shin. The conjecture over whether this injury made the difference in that star-crossed event has made its way far and wide in the Angels blogosphere.

In 1987 Joyner was outstanding, hitting a career-high 34 home runs and knocking in 117. But 1987 was a transition year for home runs; many feel the "steroid era" marks its beginnings in that season,

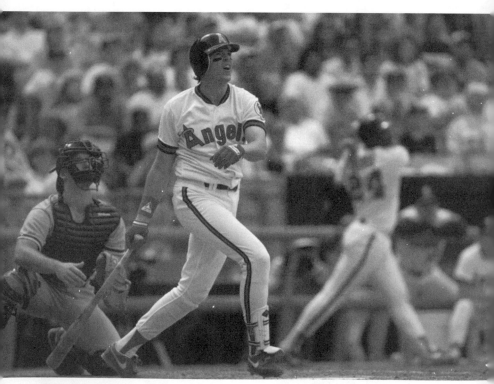

Wally Joyner came on the scene with gusto in 1986, moved on in free agency, then returned to the Angels in 2001. Photo courtesy of Getty Images.

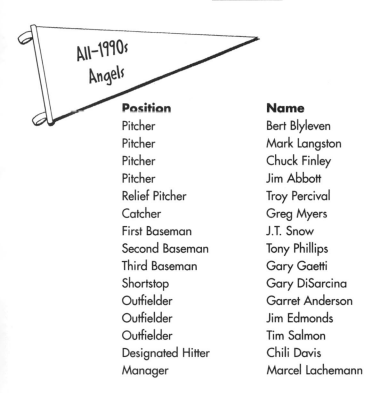

Position	Name
Pitcher	Bert Blyleven
Pitcher	Mark Langston
Pitcher	Chuck Finley
Pitcher	Jim Abbott
Relief Pitcher	Troy Percival
Catcher	Greg Myers
First Baseman	J.T. Snow
Second Baseman	Tony Phillips
Third Baseman	Gary Gaetti
Shortstop	Gary DiSarcina
Outfielder	Garret Anderson
Outfielder	Jim Edmonds
Outfielder	Tim Salmon
Designated Hitter	Chili Davis
Manager	Marcel Lachemann

in which many feel the ball was "juiced," the ballparks started to get smaller, and of course the players were getting stronger.

Thirty-four homers or not, Joyner was a gap hitter with good control of the strike zone. Joyner only hit 13 home runs in 1988, and he continued to regress in 1989. However, during a four-game series in Anaheim against the Tigers, Joyner broke a 3–3 tie in the bottom of the ninth with a single to center, scoring Claudell Washington. The next day, Detroit entered the bottom of the ninth with a 7–6 lead. Devon White singled. Joyner blasted a home run into the old bullpen to win the game.

Two days later the score was 4–4 in the bottom of the ninth when Joyner came up with the bases loaded. Brad Havens hit him with a pitch, giving him the game-winning RBI.

Joyner injured his knee in 1990 but hit .301 in 1991 while playing Gold Glove–caliber defense. At 29 he was victimized by Jackie Autry's penuriousness and the presence of Lee Stevens, who never materialized. The Royals paid him $2.1 million in 1992. To many fans

That Gary Gaetti believed in the "Angels Curse" to the extent that he wondered whether there was a secret witches' coven at Anaheim Stadium? The Curse was alive and well in the years after Donnie Moore's suicide. In 1992 the Angels' team bus careened off the New Jersey Turnpike, crashing into a wooded area in New Jersey. Manager Buck Rodgers missed most of the year with serious injuries. Chuck Finley performed heroically in saving several trapped teammates. In 1997 infielder Tony Phillips was arrested at a crack motel. His subsequent suspension probably cost the team their legitimate shot at the division title.

Joyner was "Mr. Angel." Instead of paying roughly $4 million to Wally Joyner, then-GM Whitey Herzog paid a total of $4.5 million to Von Hayes and Hubie Brooks. 'Nuff said.

He had success in Kansas City, San Diego, and Atlanta. He came back to the Angels in 2001, at the age of 39, trading in his former number 21 (then occupied by Shigetoshi Hasegawa).

He is considered to be a "Top 10 Angel" who played in relative obscurity before Tim Salmon and Troy Glaus. No Angels first baseman has approached his performance in the years since he left.

Malaise

The years after the 1986 playoff disaster were not kind to the Angels. They were years of malaise for the team and for Southern California. This had always been the Magic Kingdom, a term that once described the Southland, not just Disneyland. It described a place of possibility, a place that stood out from the rest of the world.

Hollywood, the surf craze, great moments in sports; these were the kinds of things that always defined the Southland. After the Dodgers won the 1988 World Series, however, the "curse" seemed to envelop the entire region.

In 1991 black motorist Rodney King was beaten by white Los Angeles cops. A year later, when they were acquitted, a city long thought to have "gotten it right" when it came to racial equality, exploded in flames. That was followed by the murder of O.J. Simpson's wife and O.J.'s subsequent acquittal, which further divided the city, not to mention the country. A major earthquake rocked the Southland. A stray gang bullet struck a USC football player during practice. Orange County declared bankruptcy. The Reagan-Nixon era came to an end, with political power shifting to the north.

It was no better on the field of play. USC and UCLA fell from their status as traditional powers in football. Magic Johnson's HIV status in 1991 seemed to end the whole party, and the Lakers were also-rans. The Dodgers and the Angels kept going downhill. A 1994 baseball strike sunk everything.

Buzzy Bavasi took the "Angels Curse" seriously enough to suggest a priest exorcise Anaheim Stadium of its demons. His wife convinced him he would be seen as crazy. Pitcher Chuck Finley thought it was the physical location, since the strange events had not

DID YOU KNOW . . . That 1995 Angels manager Marcel Lachemann and his brother, Rene, had played at Dorsey High School, were Dodgers batboys, and members of Rod Dedeaux's national championship team at USC? Cincinnati manager Sparky Anderson also grew up in their neighborhood, reportedly sleeping in a room that was once located where home plate at Dedeaux Field now sits.

started until the move to Orange County in 1966. Some advocated an investigation of whether the stadium was built over ancient American Indian burial grounds.

"You look at the Rams occupying this field, also," he said of a team considered football's best organization when they played at the L.A. Coliseum, then the worst when they played at the Big A, then a Super Bowl champion when they moved to St. Louis. "Maybe they were the smart ones by leaving. I understand that some bad luck goes with the game, but I'd like someone to explain to me why it goes more with our game."

If anybody (other than a priest) seemed equipped to bring good luck to the franchise, it was Disney. Thus did they step "to the rescue." Everything Walt Disney had touched—just like Gene Autry before he bought the team—had turned to gold. But if bad karma is real, perhaps Disney had made deals that would haunt them.

Walt Disney himself was a conservative who insisted that his theme park and the theme of his movies and TV programs be family-oriented. He died in 1966. The company held the line for years, but Hollywood immorality burrowed its way into the company and kept eating its way out.

The Disney Corporation that bought the Angels from a dying Gene Autry—thus unburdening his widow of accumulated baseball debts—was not the company of Walt Disney. It was the Disney of Michael Eisner, a hard-edged Hollywood agent considered the biggest power broker in a town in which lying, cheating, and stealing are art forms to be admired. Disney was no longer making family classics about kids or animals finding their way home.

In 1995, however, it looked for most of the year as if the club was blessed. The sale to Disney was in the works and it looked to be a fairy tale ending for Autry, a chance to win in his last year before riding into the credits.

Instead it was a disaster every bit as terrible as 1982 or 1986. In the pantheon of blown regular-season leads, it compares with the 1951 Dodgers, Mauch's 1964 Phillies, the 1969 Cubs, and the 1978 Red Sox.

By 1995 the three-division, wild-card format was in place. By early August the California Angels, wearing retro 1960s uniforms

Fans watch the action from the upper deck of Anaheim Stadium during an Angels and Milwaukee Brewers game in 1996. The Walt Disney Company and the city of Anaheim committed more than $100 million to a renovation of the stadium to a more compact, baseball-only facility.

By the NUMBERS **88**—Mark Langston's victory total with the Angels (fifth in team history). Not as unpopular with the fans as Jim Edmonds, he remains an enigma—talented, but his courage questioned—who had some good numbers, but never delivered to his perceived potential. He had a .543 winning percentage with 6.92 strikeouts per game, and 1,112 strikeouts in eight Angels seasons. On the day of the infamous O.J. Simpson acquittal in October 1995, Langston was smashed around while Randy Johnson dominated.

and featuring a fabulous new slugger, Tim Salmon, seemingly had the West wrapped up. Seattle was a dying baseball town in 1995. They virtually conceded the division, setting their sights on the wild-card. Their attendance was mediocre at the horrid Kingdome. A referendum was set to explore the building of what is now Safeco Field. At the time, it seemed to have as much chance as a one-legged man in a butt-kicking contest. They featured a big left-hander from the University of Southern California, Randy Johnson, who for years had looked to be a bust but had finally established himself as a dominant strikeout pitcher of Ryan-esque proportions.

Seattle whittled away at California's 10½-game lead on August 16, creating a first-place tie on September 20. It was the fastest disappearance of a 10-game lead in baseball history. With all the momentum swung to Seattle, where the town went utterly *bonkers*, the Angels actually hung in there instead of completely falling apart. They won their last five games to force a playoff at the Kingdome.

There loomed the 6'10" Johnson, who struck out 12 to make the heavy-hitting Angels look like a Little League team. It was a performance on par with Tom Seaver dominating in the 1973 playoffs or Sandy Koufax getting the Twins to swing at chin-high heat in the '65 Fall Classic. Safeco Field was built that day, the crowd in delirium in a campaign rally no politician could ever hope to match. It was not a victory but a celebration, 9–1.

"It's a very sickening feeling, and you never get over it," said Angels third-base coach Rick Burleson, who as a member of the Red Sox had been part of their blowing a 14-game lead in June of 1978. Of course, June is not *August 16*. Club president Richard Brown compared it to "watching a close friend die."

Despite the terrible disappointment, it was a talented club. Chad Curtis was traded to Detroit for Tony Phillips, who provided 27 homers. Tim Salmon hit .330 with 34 home runs and 105 runs batted in.

Center fielder Jim Edmonds, a local product from Diamond Bar, became a star in 1995: 33 home runs and 107 runs batted in. Another Orange County lad, J.T. Snow, was the son of ex-Notre Dame and Rams great Jack Snow. He was also a teammate of Marlins and Giants closer Robb Nen at Los Alamitos High School. He slammed 24 home runs and played terrific defense at first base in 1995.

L.A.-born rookie Garret Anderson (.321) was *The Sporting News* Rookie of the Year. Another Southern Californian, Troy Percival, drank 20 cups of coffee and chewed his way through four cans of Copenhagen a day. In between, the jittery fireballer blew 100 mph heat out of the bullpen.

The lefty-lefty combination of Mark Langston (15–7) and Chuck Finley (15–12) was solid but not championship solid. There were no Randy Johnsons in Anaheim. These two were a well-known combo in Anaheim. Both had blond good looks and seemed born to pitch for the Angels. Both threw hard. Both were thought to have Cy Young potential.

TRIVIA

**Who is
Rex Hudler?**

Answers to the trivia questions are on pages 189–190.

Both ultimately failed to live up to high expectations and high salaries.

Langston had come out of Buchser High School in Santa Clara. In his sophomore year at San Jose State University, he was considered the best left-handed prospect in the nation. In his junior year, he could not get anybody out.

Langston signed a free-agent contract with the Angels in 1989. He had improved from his junior year at San Jose State but was always overrated; his looks, his high radar gun readings, his left-handed arc continuing to prove a bluff.

Finley was cut out of the same cloth—a southpaw flame-thrower from the Louisiana Bayou. Their 15-win seasons on teams that gave them all the offensive support a pitcher could ask for in 1995 typify their careers and, in some ways, the Angels franchise until 2002.

General Manager Mike Brown tried to patch the rest of the staff together with a deal, but there were no legitimate stoppers attained. Langston's final-game Kingdome start was an example. Johnson, a legitimate ace, overshadowed him. He gamely hung in there, trailing 1–0 in the seventh before the roof collapsed.

Despite having the talent to come back in 1996, California folded early, as if to erase any doubt as to whether it was a team of championship caliber. The Disney deal was finalized, and mediocrity was theirs.

"The Singing Cowboy"

Gene Autry has often been referred to as a "player's owner." This goes back to the fact that, while he was a multimillionaire business success, he started out as a contract player, on the other side of the moguls who ran Hollywood in his day. In many ways, his homespun "man of the people" reputation is similar to another fellow who rose through the same system, his friend, Ronald Reagan.

Steve Bisheff, in *Tales from the Angels Dugout*, compared Autry to Pittsburgh Steelers owner Art Rooney, an apt observation. He came on the scene known as "the Singing Cowboy," a beloved horseman in a kinder, gentler time. He truly loved baseball, having grown up listening to St. Louis Cardinals games on the legendary KMOX.

Throughout his long tenure as the Angels owner, it was often uttered, "Win one for the Cowboy!" It would not be an exaggeration to suggest that Angels failures in the clutch were partially attributable to their intense desire to give the old man the ultimate triumph.

Autry was born in a tiny Texas town in 1907. His story is the story of America. There are very few famous and successful men in other countries with backgrounds as humble as the many famous and successful Americans who, by pursuing the American Dream, attain greatness. There is little real explanation for it. Democracy, capitalism, freedom, the pioneer spirit, the immigrant success story—these are all offered as reasons, and each may be valid.

Autry seems to be one of those fortunate men. Autry worked hard, to be sure. He worked as a railroad telegraph operator at 18, and in the boredom of the long hours began to strum a guitar.

"Just so I had something to strum on," he said.

He got good enough at it. In 1934 he was convinced that the future lay out West, so he packed his bags, blowing into Hollywood with his guitar and little else. Three years later he was a movie star known as "the Singing Cowboy." Many people have heard the song "Rudolph the Red-Nosed Reindeer." Autry made it famous.

With big paychecks came astute business sense. Autry quickly developed himself into a franchise. He bought radio stations, which of course played his songs, which in turn made him richer. He sang his way into the movie hearts of millions.

In 1960 he went to St. Louis to buy the rights to broadcast Los Angeles Dodgers games. Having just purchased KMPC in Los Angeles, he wanted to get the Dodgers back. Walter O'Malley had left Autry's Golden West Broadcasting Network and switched to KFI.

Charlie O. Finley and several others were deemed unsuitable for ownership of the new American League franchise in L.A. Autry, in the right place at the right time, was approached, agreed to make a bid, and found his $1.5 million letter of credit to be satisfactory. He owned the Angels.

Beloved owner Gene Autry arrives at an owners meeting in Los Angeles in 1996. At the meeting owners approved the sale of a controlling interest in the Angels to the Walt Disney Company.

"First time in baseball history a franchise has been awarded to a horse," wrote New York columnist Red Smith in reference to Autry's equine movie sidekick.

TRIVIA

Who was Jim "Hollywood" Edmonds traded for?

Answers to the trivia questions are on pages 189–190.

After the great success of 1962, Autry and the Angels fans thought pennants would follow. Disappointment, however, mostly dogged Autry and his team. It was in the face of failure that Autry developed a love, admiration, and respect that "winners" like Finley and George Steinbrenner never did. Leo Durocher once said, "Nice guys finish last," but there is much evidence to dispute this theory. Autry usually did not finish last, he just never finished first.

Of course, he finished first in the American League West a few times, but never the ultimate "first," a Series title or at least an appearance in the fall classic. Autry was always philosophical.

"In the movies, I never lost a fight," he once said. "In baseball, I hardly ever won one."

From day one, he used to come down and hang around with the players, said ex-catcher and manager Buck Rodgers: "[Jim] Fregosi and me, we were just kids, but we'd sit around after a game, drink beer for 45 minutes and listen to the cowboy tell stories. He was very personable, very concerned about our welfare."

"I don't think anyone ever had a bad thing to say about Mr. Autry," said Dean Chance. "He was simply a wonderful, nice person. And he really did love baseball. You could tell that just by sitting and talking with him. But he never stuck his nose in. He didn't try to be a pushy owner. The great thing was, he seemed like just one of the guys."

"I think what struck you about him," said Bobby Knoop, "is that for someone so successful and wealthy, he was such a kind and humble man. He never criticized us, even when we had a bad season. He was just a friend. Even though he was our owner and our boss, whenever he was around, he made you feel he was there for us, not that we were supposed to be there for him."

Autry was friends with three former presidents. Dwight Eisenhower was a resident of Palm Springs, where the Angels trained. He played golf with Autry, attended Angels exhibition

145

By the NUMBERS In 2000, Darin Erstad threatened to break the all-time record for most hits in a season, but fell short with 240. George Sisler set the record of 257 with the 1920 Browns. Ichiro Suzuki of Seattle finally broke the mark in 2004 when he garnered 262 hits.

games, and even sat in the dugout once, when Bill Rigney let him call the shots for an inning.

Autry was close to Richard Nixon, who was born in Orange County, established the "Western White House" in San Clemente, and helped rehab his image in large part through his frequent appearances at Anaheim Stadium in 1979.

Autry also knew Ronald Reagan, who like himself was from the heartland and had blown into Hollywood and made good. Reagan was very popular in Orange County.

Autry's screen horse was named Champion. His first wife, Ina, was the love of his life until she passed away. His second wife, Jackie, was 34 years his junior.

Autry's greatest concern regarding baseball's economics was that it would make it beyond the ability of average families to attend games. He knew that the key to the game's success came through the kids.

Despite his anguish over tough losses, he always handled those disappointments with class and dignity. He called his players "the boys," never holding it against them if they failed to come through.

"I don't know, I've never considered myself a legend or anything like that," he was quoted saying by *Orange County Register* sportswriter Steve Bisheff. "I've loved everything that I did. I loved radio. I was happy when I was making movies and records. They're all favorites of mine. I tried to pick songs that would be record sellers. Sometimes I'd hit and sometimes I'd miss. I was pretty lucky. I had a lot more hits than misses."

When Autry would be carted out before the Anaheim Stadium fans, wearing his 10-gallon hat, he would smile and wave.

"I feel like I'm back in the saddle again," he would say.

Autry passed in 1998. When the club won the World Series in 2002, it was dedicated to his memory.

Deliverance

For 40 years the Angels wandered in the desert of modern Los Angeles. They were led by a "Singing Cowboy," a "White Rat," a "Smiling Python," and a "Little General."

The hourglass of time, however, seemed to usher in with the new millennium a new age of sports redemption. It happened in Boston. It happened in Chicago. In Los Angeles a football team called the Trojans, once the playground of gridiron gods, found that they were once again. Just down the freeway, the Angels discovered deliverance; deliverance from the pharaohic Dodgers, who no longer held sway over the deserts, canyons, and vistas of the Southland. After changing the color scheme to red, the new-style Angels were delivered to a Promised Land called the World Championship. The brass ring.

Like David's chances when he first set out against Goliath, or Moses's first efforts to set his people free, it did not start out in a promising manner. Of all the teams thought to be contenders in 2002, the Angels were far from being on the top of anyone's list. In the National League, of course, were the Giants, who featured a modern Goliath named Barry Bonds, the most dangerous offensive threat the game had ever seen. There were the defending world champions, the Diamondbacks. They had Curt Schilling and an old Angels killer, Randy Johnson. The Cardinals and Braves were certainly in the discussion.

In their own league the Yankees, who had lost by the slimmest of margins the previous fall, straddled the landscape in a manner as dominant as their Ruth-DiMaggio-Mantle past. The American League West was a barbed encampment the Angels would have to fight their way out of if they hoped to even think about these other behemoths: two champions in their primes rendered the division the imprimatur of "best in baseball."

The favorite? Take your pick. The Oakland A's, winners of 102 games, had the best starting pitching in baseball plus power, defense, and confidence. They had ridden their wild-card to dominance over the Yankees until God seemingly touched New York in the wake of 9/11, replacing dread with excitement, victory clutched from hopelessness.

This team of All-Stars, however, had not sniffed Seattle in the 2001 regular season. Japanese import Ichiro Suzuki sparked the Mariners to a start like none before. They never looked back. The Mariners were not just good. They had people saying they might be the best team of *all time!* They could afford to drop 16 games off their pace and still catch the century mark.

If the Angels thought the spring training move from Palm Springs to Tempe would redirect them from their swinging past to a greater focus on baseball fundamentals, they might have noticed the changing demographics of desert life. Palm Springs, once the bikini-clad playground of Bo Belinsky, was now more of an old folks home. Tempe is the home of Arizona State University, designated by no less an authority than *Playboy* magazine to be the national champion of collegiate hotties. Right next door is a town called Scottsdale. Once a geriatric golf community, it now possesses a *Girls Gone Wild* nightlife, prompting A's pitcher Tim Hudson to say of Spring Training in this environment: "We gotta get outta this town while we're still standing."

Whether the deadly Tempe-Scottsdale combo had anything to do with it or not is just speculation, but the Angels started out the 2002 campaign as if they had spent the month training at Martini Ranch. Questions abounded, chief among them being whether Darin Erstad and Tim Salmon could return to form. Salmon was now a veteran .290 career hitter who had averaged 30 homers and 100 RBIs but in 2001 had hit .227 with 17 home runs and 49 RBIs.

Erstad, possibly the best athlete on a team of great all-around athletes, slumped from a spectacular year in 2000 (.355, 25 HRs, 100 RBIs) to .258 in 2001.

There seemed little reason to even care much when Anaheim lost 14 of its first 20 games. The A's, notorious for their slow starts, were too talented to play poorly, warm weather or not. Seattle looked poised to pick up where they had left off in 2001.

Toward the end of April, the season threatened to run away from them. On April 24 at Safeco Field, however, Anaheim won a key 10–6 game over Seattle. Scott Spiezio's three-run double and Tim Salmon's first homer of the year gave left-hander Jarrod Washburn

With the World Series championship trophy at left, Anaheim Angels manager Mike Scioscia talks to thousands of cheering fans during the celebration of the Angels' 2002 World Series championship at Edison International Field in Anaheim. From left are Troy Glaus, Scott Spiezio, and pitcher John Lackey.

By the NUMBERS

$100 million—Cost of renovating Anaheim Stadium into Edison International Field of Anaheim beginning in 1998. The Big A had been converted into a football-baseball facility in 1981, but the Rams left Anaheim in 1995. Part of the Disney purchase of the mid-1990s included rebuilding the stadium into a baseball-only arena, with the Edison Corporation, a major energy conglomerate, taking on the costs. When Arte Moreno took over ownership, the facility was thankfully renamed Angels Stadium.

a much-needed victory. It broke a six-game 2002 losing streak to division-leading Seattle and a four-game losing skein. It got them on the right track.

Reliever Troy Percival regained his old form. A rookie, Francisco Rodriguez, emerged. A diminutive shortstop, David Eckstein, hit a grand slam to give Anaheim a 14-inning win over Toronto. On May 3 at SkyDome, Anaheim captured their eighth straight win.

"Our goal isn't to play .500 baseball," said Erstad, whose three-run homer keyed the win. "We plan on being much better than that."

On May 8, all-everything third baseman Troy Glaus broke a season-long slump with his first homer at home since 2001 to key a 3–2 win over Detroit behind Kevin Appier and Troy Percival at Edison Field. Salmon's May 25 homer keyed their 22nd win in 26 games, 4–3 over Minnesota. The league had taken notice. Garret Anderson's two-run double was the difference in a 4–3 victory over Cincinnati on June 7 that elevated Anaheim to within a game of first place.

It was still early, though. Everybody waited for Seattle to make their move, Oakland to turn on the afterburners, Anaheim to fade. By July there was no fade to be found. Washburn won his 11th straight decision, 4–2 over the Twins at the Metrodome. The club returned to Orange County, where baseball fever had swept the region. Anaheim knocked the Dodgers around in interleague play, "announcing," as Nuke LaLoosh once said in *Bull Durham*, their regional "presence with authority." They were in the middle of a crowded first-place fight with the West-leading Mariners, just ahead of Oakland.

Seattle would be the first to fall, and it was Anaheim who gave them the push. Washburn's 12th straight win completed a home sweep of the M's, 7–5. On July 24, they let Oakland know they had no plans to lay down against the mighty A's, with Aaron Sele beating Tim Hudson 5–1.

A 1–0 Angels squeaker behind Appier over Seattle on July 28 gave them false hope that maybe...

Then it happened. With Seattle slowly sinking in the West, the juggernaut A's asserted themselves like the American Army at the Meuse-Argonne. As if to say, "Okay, no more screwin' around," Oakland took control of August and early September, winning a league-record *20 consecutive games*, thus providing all the reality check the Angels needed to knock their fragile psyches around like a rag doll.

It was time to congratulate themselves on "a job well done," "close but no cigar," and "maybe next year." Choose the platitude from a menu of previous statements describing good Angels teams and disappointing finishes in 1979, 1982, 1986, and 1995.

Except this was the new millennium. The old witching hour was no more. Dorothy would capture the broom this time. The team would continue to announce their "presence with authority."

At first the Oakland romp played itself out for what it looked to be— the separation of boys from men. About halfway through their streak, however, the green and gold began to take troubling note of the fact that no matter how much ordnance they

TRIVIA

Darin Erstad was an All-American college football player. What school did he attend?

Answers to the trivia questions are on pages 189–190.

laid on their opponents, they remained alive and well to win another day. Seattle could not handle the Oakland run, but Anaheim did. Very well.

Meaningful September baseball was played up and down the West Coast. San Francisco was storming along, riding the unstoppable Barry Bonds. But day after day, Oakland's wins were matched by equally impressive Anaheim victories. On September 1, while the A's won their 18th straight, Anaheim knocked off Baltimore 9–3 to remain three and a half back. A week later they had a 10-game winning streak. Glaus's two homers and Washburn's mound work keyed a 6–2 pasting of the Orioles at Camden Yards. Next up: four games with Oakland.

If the A's thought the next week would be a replay of Alexander's conquest of the mysterious East, they felt more like Romans watching Hannibal march within sight of their gates. After a 1–0 victory over Oakland at Network Associates Coliseum, Anaheim claimed *sole possession* of first place. The game was won on a dramatic ninth-inning homer by Salmon off Oakland reliever Billy Koch.

"I've never been to the playoffs, but I can't imagine anything much more adrenaline-filled than this," said Percival after closing out the game. He had finally found an effective substitute for his old "20 cups of coffee and four cans of Copenhagen" routine.

The A's continued to play Rome to the Angels' Hannibal after that, however. As if by attrition, the A's hung on, keeping the barbarian invader from ultimately knocking the gates down. Anaheim roamed the countryside, looking for a way to break the final defenses. In the end, a four-game losing streak denied them the West Division championship. The wild-card setup, established eight years earlier, gave them all the life they still needed, however.

"I had a glimpse of it my first year, but that has been a sour note in my career until now," Anderson said after the 10–5 win over Texas on September 26 clinched a postseason berth.

Mike Scioscia

Mike Scioscia is the youngest of three children. His father, Fred, ran a beer distributorship, and his mother, Florence, was a teacher. Scioscia grew up in Morton, Pennsylvania. It was his parents' work ethic that drove him to succeed even though he may not have had the greatest natural tools.

"I remember playing sports my whole life," Scioscia said. "One of my first memories is running around playing with friends and playing ball when I was three or four years old. We played ice hockey, baseball, football, and basketball. Everything was seasonal back East."

Scioscia played baseball, basketball, and football at Springfield High. He was named Delaware County Player of the Year in 1975 and 1976. His first love, however, was Penn State football.

"A recruiter said I was too small and too slow for guys at that level," he said.

Several baseball scholarships were in the offing when the Dodgers made Scioscia the 19th overall pick in the 1976 draft. Clemson offered a football scholarship.

"My mom taught for 30 years, so she supported going to Clemson," he recalled in Joe Haakenson's *Out of the Blue.* "My dad said it might be my only opportunity to play pro ball. They were split, and it was up to me."

Scioscia was contemplating his options when he got a phone call from Tom Lasorda, who was the Dodgers' third-base coach and would, by season's end, be named manager. L.A. was in town to play the Phillies—Lasorda is a native of nearby Norristown, Pennsylvania—and he said somebody would be by to pick him up to bring him to Veterans Stadium for a workout.

Shown in a 2006 photo, Mike Scioscia has been the manager for the Angels since the 2000 season.

That cinched it. The Dodgers liked what they saw, and Scioscia bought into the Dodger Way, no doubt via Lasorda's sell job. He was on a plane to Bellingham, Washington, the next day. His mother got what she wanted, however, by insisting the club pay for his college education. He did end up attending the University of Delaware from 1976 to 1978.

In 1979 Scioscia had a big year at Triple A Albuquerque, where he hit .336 with 34 doubles. He broke into the major leagues catching Rick Sutcliffe on April 20, 1980, and at first split time with veteran Steve Yeager. Scioscia's early years coincided with the great "Fernandomania" phenomenon of Mexican-born pitching sensation Fernando Valenzuela.

"The whole thing was a bunch of things coming together at the right time," said Scioscia. "He was an incredible talent, and he was pitching in a city that was just waiting for someone like him to come out of Mexico. It was exciting for all of Southern California, not just the Mexican community. I was just 22 and he was just 20...it was a unique experience."

In 1981 Scisocia helped lead Los Angeles to the world championship. His teammate on that team was Dusty Baker, whom he would square off against as manager in the 2002 World Series.

Throughout the 1980s, Scioscia was a mainstay behind the plate. It was a strange decade in Dodgers history. They had a number of down years, yet won the World Series twice. The 1988 title was memorable, with Scioscia handling the pitching offerings of the unbelievable Orel Hershiser, who got on a hot streak unmatched in history (59 straight shutout innings).

Unfortunately, Scioscia was not behind the plate in Game 5 of the '88 Series, when Hershiser closed out the A's at Oakland. He had injured himself and was unavailable.

Scioscia was a National League All-Star in 1989 and 1990, but injuries forced him to the sidelines by 1993. He became a minor league coach for L.A. When former teammate Bill Russell was named manager in 1997, Scioscia came on board as a bench coach. Over the next couple seasons, turmoil enveloped the once-proud Dodgers. The transition from the O'Malley family to Fox was followed by a string of firings. Scioscia was passed over as a big-league manager, so he decided to go to Triple A.

The Dodgers' general manager at that time was the embattled Kevin Malone.

"I was wondering where the organization was going, if they could give me an idea," Scioscia recalled. "He said there were many things in transition that...weren't clear. I thought the best thing for me was to get out early and give myself the opportunity to look for some spots."

Scioscia was not desperate, however. He turned down interviews with Tampa Bay and the White Sox.

TRIVIA

Who starred in the movie *Angels in the Outfield*?

Answers to the trivia questions are on pages 189–190.

Scioscia's stock rose, and in late 1999, when Bill Stoneman took over as Anaheim's general manager, he hired Scioscia to take over the club. Fred Claire, a longtime Dodgers executive, highly recommended him. The choice turned out to be a rock solid one, with the world championship coming in his third year on the job.

By the NUMBERS **8**—The number of Hall of Famers who have worn an Angels uniform. These include Rod Carew, Reggie Jackson, Frank Robinson, Hoyt Wilhelm, Don Sutton, Eddie Murray, and Nolan Ryan.

There is no question that the 2002 Angels were a talented club, but Scioscia's handling of them was nothing less than masterful. First, they were not favored in what was the best division in baseball. The Mariners and A's were heavy favorites to finish ahead of them. With little expected of the Angels, they delivered little in April (a 6–14 start), but the manager refused to let the team get down on themselves. He steered them to a 10-game winning streak.

Then, when the A's threatened to run away with it, Anaheim hung tough. The club certainly scored a lot of runs, but Scioscia's handling of the pitching staff—his career as a catcher came in handy—won it. The Angels were a "pitching staff by committee," using starters for five or six innings then turning things over to a hard-throwing bullpen that needed to be handled just right.

There were shaky personalities in that Angels pen—youngsters, veterans, and in-betweens. They all contributed perfectly. Scioscia deserves the greatest credit.

Yankee Killers

The nature of major league baseball is one of second chances and endless obstacles. Winning it all is, as Jason Giambi said, "a marathon." Unlike college football, where a single loss can derail a team's chances at the national championship, baseball offers its participants many chances at redemption. A long season is filled with losses and the opportunity to rebound from them. The good teams do not let the losses mount.

Pro football offers a playoff system—but lose one of those games and it is suddenly wintertime. The big-league ballclub has survived a long, grueling course, starting in February when they report to spring training, yet for those still alive the biggest challenge does not come until October. Oh, October, a month of magic and black magic—a Halloween trick...or treat?

The Angels knew this month well. The 2002 version might have hoped that they were not part of the old Angels of flops and foibles, but they had their veterans from the fall of 1995: Salmon, Anderson, and Percival.

Now, the baseball gods seemed to have played another trick on them. One by one, more bricks had been lain in that big obstacle built specifically, it seemed, to hold them back. Once all a team had to do was win the league. Then they had to win a division and a three-of-five playoff; then a four-of-seven playoff. Every test had been failed.

Now, the Anaheim Angels, a wild-card team playing without home-field advantage, would have to get past a three-of-five Divisional Series, then a League Championship Series, and only then would an invite to the big dance be extended.

Oh, and by the way, the festivities began against the New York Yankees at Yankee Stadium. Now the Angels, convincing themselves the Yanks can be beaten, like to say that Babe Ruth and Whitey Ford are not wearing pinstripes when they take the field. They are wrong. Their ghosts *are* there, and they possess human powers. No, *super-human* powers. If you look hard enough you can see them, hittin' the long ball, knockin' the eyelash off a fly from 60'6". They are there as surely as they guide footballs into the waiting arms of Irish pass catchers, carry the pigskin for Troy at the Coliseum, sink threes for the Celtics.

Can they be beaten? Yes, but only by "Dandy Sandy" on his best day, Vince Young on winged feet, Magic Johnson at his most inspired.

Thus did the Anaheim Angels enter the challenge of greatness on October 1, 2002, at the corner of East 161st Street and River Avenue, Bronx, New York. With no time to waste in a short series, the Angels folded like an accordion. All their fabulous accomplishments, their *mano a mano* death struggles with Oakland, were to be deposited into the dustbin of history via a patented Yankees stomping, with a little Angels angst just for good measure.

Washburn had nothing. It was 5–4 Angels in the eighth, but of course the seasoned baseball observer knew that Frank Sinatra was already singing "New York, New York." Manager Mike Scioscia entered that long pantheon known as second-guessed Angels managers when he chose to go with journeyman Scott Schoeneweis against superstar Jason Giambi, instead of bringing in the dominant Percival.

Naturally, the move backfired—followed by a collapse worthy of a certain piece of communist-era Berlin architecture: 8–5, Yankees.

At this point the dissection of the Angels reveals something new. Their cursed 20th-century past always came via an agonizing come-from-ahead fall, filled with moral recriminations. But this was a hole, dug into the Yankee Stadium turf, and little was expected after Game 1. With nothing expected, suddenly the old coat of shame was lighter.

The Angels pile onto the field to celebrate their 9–5 victory over the New York Yankees to win their American League Division Series in Anaheim on October 5, 2002.

DID YOU KNOW ... That prior to Major League Baseball coming to Los Angeles, the Angels' PCL franchise won 14 league titles between 1905 and 1957?

Because nothing *was* expected, they suddenly seemed free to explode early off Andy Pettitte to take a 4–0 lead. Then came that demarcation point separating everything anybody knows about Angels baseball prior to 2002 with everything known about them since then.

Act II on the Stadium stage featured tragedy worthy of *King Lear*. The box score cannot do justice to the *sound* of Yankee Stadium when their heroes roar back like gangbusters breaking up the rackets. Five runs and a 5–4 Yankees lead through six had the Bronx in full throttle. The Angels stood before them like dumbfounded *Wehrmacht*, while Patton's tanks rolled over them on the road to Berlin.

Act III was not the Bard's. Think more of Mark I, 28:1–20. You can look it up.

The resurrection at Yankee Stadium on October 2, 2002, began in the form of Garret Anderson's tying eighth-inning homer off of Orlando Hernandez. Still, with the score tied on the other guy's turf, it looked like smiles, followed by impending disappointment, followed by inevitable disaster.

"Oh, ye of little faith."

Troy Glaus changed the very *nature* of Angels baseball—its history, its character, its future—when he followed Anderson with a go-ahead shot, turning the screaming maniacs that inhabit the cacophonous stadium into stunned silence. The sound of friends and family, of Glaus's teammates, pierced the air.

It may not have been a comeback quite comparable to you-know-who, but the point is made. After blowing the lead in Game 1, Scioscia was about to make the same mistake twice. Percival was brought in to protect the lead in the bottom of the eighth, pitched out of a jam, and Anaheim breathed one giant sigh of relief, boarding the plane home tied at one with an 8–6 win.

The scene shifted to the California sunshine, where Rally Monkeys, Thunder Sticks, and red shirts suddenly made Edison Field look like a Nebraska Cornhuskers game. The Yankees have always made a specialty of entering such a festive atmosphere, breaking it up in the manner of an imperial ruler clamping down on the restless natives. It sure looked that way when the Bombers exploded for six runs in the first three innings. Instead of sitting back and taking it, the Anaheim faithful begged and pleaded. Their heroes were in full October heat, responding with two runs in the bottom of the third to claw back in. From that point on, John Lackey, Scott Schoeneweis, Francisco Rodriguez, and Troy Percival did their best imitations of Christy Mathewson.

Rodriguez in particular made his debut on the national stage. The 20-year-old rookie dominated New York bats with four strike-outs, setting it up in the seventh and eighth.

Anaheim tied it in the seventh. The home-field edge and strong bullpen gave them the mental advantage they needed. Darin Erstad's liner over Jason Giambi's head scored the go-ahead run. After that, it was "party time" in a 9–6 win.

The old "Yes, we can!" was hopeful, but now it was more like "Yes, we will!" Washburn held New York to one earned run through five in the fourth game, then turned it over to what the world now acknowledged was one of the great bullpens in recent years. Brendan Donnelly, so effective all year, gave up a couple, but Rodriguez was untouchable again with his big kick, high heat, and *yak* slider. Percival closed it out.

TRIVIA

What is the "Rally Monkey"?

Answers to the trivia questions are on pages 189–190.

David Wells, a big-game pitcher, was unable to stem the Anaheim offense. In Game 5 the Halos scored eight runs to erase a 2–1 Yankees edge. It was all over but the shouting, although there was plenty of that.

"They brought out the whuppin' stick," said Wells after the 9–5 Angels victory.

"If they keep playing the way they're playing, no one is going to beat them," said Yankees shortstop Derek Jeter.

Anaheim hit .376 against the vaunted Yankees staff of Roger Clemens, Andy Pettitte, Mike Mussina, David Wells, and of course *their* famed bullpen, which included Orlando Hernandez and the legendary Mariano Rivera.

Team of Destiny

Beating the New York Yankees in October is the biggest accomplishment in sports. There is no greater dynasty, no more formidable history to overcome. Not beating Notre Dame in South Bend, the Celtics in the Garden, the Pack at Lambeau Field—no obstacle is greater. The 2002 Yankees were at their most daunting. They had won three straight world championships and four of five between 1996 and 2000. The Yanks had lost by the thinnest of margins in 2001.

Someday, historians will conclude that the war on terror was actually won when the Yankees thrilled New York and America, creating a celebration of life after Osama Bin Laden had tried unsuccessfully to turn "Fun City's" residents into cowards afraid to open their doors. Instead, sellout crowds accorded wild standing ovations to President George W. Bush and Mayor Rudolph Giuliani.

However, having beaten something with so much history and *gravitas* attached to it could have made it easy for the Angels to let up. After years in which the "rivalry" with Oakland was a one-sided affair, finally in '02 the Angels asserted themselves. A showdown with the powerhouse A's might have seemed to be the logical next step, but competition has a way of defying logic. Perhaps because they were looking forward to the Yankees or the Angels, and the World Series, Oakland seemingly failed to recognize that the Minnesota Twins were a first-class baseball club. It was the Metrodome, not Network Associates Coliseum that was the next destination of a club thinking maybe they were a team of destiny.

The Metrodome is a "house of horrors" most of the time, anyway. When the Twins have a good ballclub, then it can be a graveyard. They had ridden home-field advantage to maximum effectiveness in beating St. Louis in the 1987 World Series, then repeating the trick against Atlanta in 1991.

The Angels entered the dome expecting to score a lot of runs, as they were hot as a pistol. They also figured they would need every one of those runs. They were mostly wrong. They did not score much, but they did not need a lot. The run they did score, however, fell two shy of what they did need in a 2–1 Minnesota win.

The Angels celebrate on the field after winning Game 5 of the American League Championship Series against the Minnesota Twins in Anaheim on October 13, 2002. The Angels won the game 13–5 to advance to the World Series. At front center, Tim Salmon hugs David Eckstein.

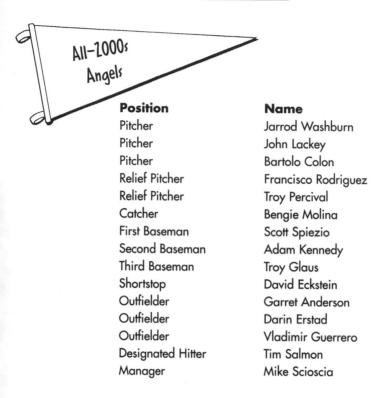

All-2000s Angels

Position	Name
Pitcher	Jarrod Washburn
Pitcher	John Lackey
Pitcher	Bartolo Colon
Relief Pitcher	Francisco Rodriguez
Relief Pitcher	Troy Percival
Catcher	Bengie Molina
First Baseman	Scott Spiezio
Second Baseman	Adam Kennedy
Third Baseman	Troy Glaus
Shortstop	David Eckstein
Outfielder	Garret Anderson
Outfielder	Darin Erstad
Outfielder	Vladimir Guerrero
Designated Hitter	Tim Salmon
Manager	Mike Scioscia

The Twins, fresh off beating Oakland, had a habit of winning when they got to October. This time it looked to be at the considerable expense of the Angels, who threatened to go flat in the wake of beating the vaunted Yankees.

The Metrodome myth was partially wiped away, however, when Anaheim responded with a 6–3 Game 2 triumph behind home runs by Erstad and Brad Fullmer.

Glaus's eighth-inning homer broke up a pitcher's duel started by Eric Milton and Washburn; Rodriguez and Percival were perfect in the eighth and ninth. The Angels took the third contest by 2–1.

John Lackey and veteran Brad Radke went at it in another pitcher's duel, but Anaheim's guns were too potent. It was Glaus again, with a go-ahead single in the seventh, to key the 7–1 win.

Now the pressure was on to wrap it up at home. Nobody wanted to see the Metrodome until 2003. After what had happened to Anaheim in 1982 and 1986, the "one game away" scenario was on everybody's minds. If they lost, they would have two more chances, but their wild-card status meant Games 6 and 7 would require an unwanted trip to the Metrodome. The Angels made quick work of the old bugaboos, however.

"I know Mr. Autry's smiling up there, and I'm so happy that Jackie's here to enjoy it with us," Tim Salmon said after a 13–5 Angels win, leaving no doubt.

This time the hero was Adam Kennedy, a local kid from Cal State Northridge, who hit a three-run homer off Johan Santana to put Anaheim ahead 6–5. After that it was "Katy bar the door."

"They're on a roll," Minnesota manager Ron Gardenhire said afterward.

DID YOU KNOW . . . That Scott Spiezio's father, Ed Spiezio, played nine years in the major leagues for St. Louis, San Diego, and the Chicago White Sox from 1964 to 1972, appearing in the 1967 and 1968 World Series?

The Quiet Man

Tim Salmon was the John Wayne of the Angels. On a team known throughout its history for playboys, party animals, colorful characters, and recalcitrants, he more resembled Wayne's character in *The Quiet Man*. He was strong, never complained, and was always reliable.

Salmon came from Arizona. For many years Salmon looked to be one of those players who achieves stardom but never wins the ultimate championship, like Ernie Banks. When he came up, he found the idea of hexes and curses to be ridiculous, but after 1995 he was not so sure. He saw Gary DeSarcina break his thumb in the heat of a September pennant chase. He saw Chuck Finley suffer strange injuries. He saw a 10½-game lead disappear faster than any 10½-game lead in baseball history.

He became a starting outfielder in 1993, when he won the American League Rookie of the Year award. Salmon organized chapel for the club, providing stability in the clubhouse. He was married with four kids.

"Timmy's not only a professional, but he's an extremely talented professional," said Scioscia. "That combination is tremendous. Tim makes every player around him better."

"I always felt if you had a chance to stay in the same place your whole career, it would be something special," Salmon said of his decision to remain an Angel instead of signing with the hometown D'backs. "It's like in college where you have an alma mater. It's something you're behind. That's what I have with the Angels. I really feel it's part of my family. I look around and see coaches I saw when I was in A ball scuffling. It's nice to have those long-lasting relationships."

2002 Angels Lineup

Position	Name
Pitcher	Jarrod Washburn
Pitcher	John Lackey
Pitcher	Kevin Appier
Pitcher	Ramon Ortiz
Relief Pitcher	Francisco Rodriguez
Relief Pitcher	Brendan Donnelly
Relief Pitcher	Ben Webber
Relief Pitcher	Troy Percival
Catcher	Bengie Molina
First Baseman	Scott Spiezio
Second Baseman	Adam Kennedy
Third Baseman	Troy Glaus
Shortstop	David Eckstein
Outfielder	Garret Anderson
Outfielder	Darin Erstad
Outfielder	Tim Salmon
Designated Hitter	Brad Fullmer
Manager	Mike Scioscia

When Anaheim made it to the 2002 playoffs, Salmon had waited 1,388 games to get there—the longest number of games of any player at that time.

"I tell these young guys now, 'Just appreciate it, man. Make the most of the moment,'" Salmon was quoted saying in *Tales from the Angels Dugout.* "That's the biggest thing...be aggressive. Don't go home thinking you left anything or held anything back."

In Game 3 of the 2002 Divisional Series against New York, Anaheim trailed 6–1 when the Angels made their comeback. Salmon capped it when he got hold of Steve Karsay's hanging curve, knocking a two-run home run over the left-field fence to give his team the 9–6 win.

"I had goose bumps," he said. "I couldn't believe the crowd noise. You would have thought we'd won the seventh game of the World Series."

Salmon was 34 in 2002. He had consistently come through with 30-homer, 90-RBI years.

After losing the opener of the World Series to San Francisco, it was Salmon who spurred Anaheim's big win with a 4-for-4 game, including two home runs. His two-run clout in the eighth was the difference in an 11–10 win.

"I've been joking with him that he's been looking like he's 12 years old in the playoffs," said Darin Erstad. "After he hit that last home run, he looked like he was eight."

When Anaheim came back in Game 6 after trailing 5–0 against Russ Ortiz, Salmon followed Erstad's leadoff eighth-inning jack with

Tim Salmon discusses his retirement from baseball prior to a September 2006 game against the Oakland Athletics in Anaheim.

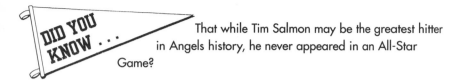

a single, leading to more runs. The next night, with victory secure, Salmon was the one who made sure to recall Gene Autry. He paraded the trophy around the field, accepting Autry's cowboy hat from Jackie Autry.

"It's all so amazing, so unbelievable, I can't even begin to describe my emotions," Salmon said afterward. "I think there's a lot of things I'm not going to really realize until later."

Salmon was thought to be washed up by some after his 2001 performance, in which he hit only .227 with 17 homers and 49 runs batted in.

"It's been really sweet, especially since we've been close a few times, had some tough collapses," he said. "It's been real nice to get there; it's been a great year."

It was the comeback of not just Salmon but veteran teammate Erstad that fueled the '02 Angels.

"They've been huge," said Scioscia. "If you look at why we're in this position, I would have to say it's been our pitching staff. To support the pitching, we needed some key guys in our lineup to rebound. None were more key than what Darin Erstad and Tim Salmon did for our club."

It was the veteran leadership of Salmon and Erstad, giving the team stability in the face of a 2–19 finish to the 2001 campaign followed up by the 6–14 2002 start. Salmon hit only .183 in April but was experienced enough to shake it off.

"I think the patience to see this lineup get together and play was what was needed," said the manager. "They certainly did after that 6–14 start; they've been incredible."

Salmon had previously considered leaving the Angels, but the club rewarded his performance with a four-year, $40 million contract.

"When I re-signed, I saw the groundwork for a pretty good club," he told John Nadel of the Associated Press.

Hero

The first thing anybody noticed when observing the 2002 Angels taking batting practice was the size of the team. This is not what baseball players used to look like. This team, like many others in the modern era, was filled with tall, big, extremely muscular men.

Now, five years after the 2002 dream year, we have seen new revelations regarding Barry Bonds's use of steroids, the BALCO scandal, and the widespread use of performance-enhancing drugs. We now know that steroid use benefits baseball players, and not just sluggers. Pitchers use it because it makes them stronger, throw harder, and recover faster.

Athletes in sports like tennis are using steroids. It is not a drug that only benefits football linemen and bodybuilders, which was the myth people held onto for a long time.

None of this says that Troy Glaus or any of his Angels teammates were on steroids in 2002. What it does say is that everybody is now under suspicion, whether innocent or not. That is the nature and unfortunate by-product of the scandal.

Glaus came up a 6'5", 245-pound third baseman possessing the most extraordinary talents. He emerged from north San Diego County, choosing to pursue his education at UCLA instead of going directly into professional ball. He may very well be the greatest baseball player in Bruins history, which is saying something. Jackie Robinson and Chris Chambliss played in Westwood.

In 2002 Glaus got off to a slow start but finished with 30 home runs and 111 runs batted in. So great was his talent and expectations for him, however, that those numbers were considered disappointing, at least until the World Series.

In 2000 and 2001, Glaus combined for 88 home runs.

"Troy's ceiling is amazing," said Scioscia. "I think he has more upside than anybody else in this clubhouse."

After winning the MVP award for the 2002 World Series, Glaus announced, "It's a great honor. But this is for the team, not for me. All 25 guys on this roster contributed to our winning."

In 16 2002 postseason games, Glaus hit seven homers. He was impossible to pitch to. No scouting report could determine his

Troy Glaus smacks a two-run double to score the go-ahead run in the eighth inning against the San Francisco Giants during Game 6 of the World Series in Anaheim on October 26, 2002.

By the NUMBERS

.846—Troy Glaus's slugging percentage in the 2002 World Series. In a battle of offensive titans, Barry Bonds's slugging percentage was an incredible 1.295 with four homers and a .471 average.

weaknesses because, when he got hot, he had none. Up and in? He tomahawked it. Away? He used his power to hit opposite-field dingers. A mistake pitch? Forget about it.

Glaus was a streaky hitter who in midseason was having trouble making contact. He struck out 29 times in 89 at-bats at one point, mainly because he insisted on trying to pull the ball. He was not using his size and massive strength. But Glaus never let his slump prevent him from giving it all he had.

"He's got a great work ethic," said hitting instructor Mickey Hatcher. "In fact, sometimes I have to get him to back off a bit. The thing is, he gets down on himself. He's been put in that category of a superstar, and it really hurts him when he feels he's not helping the team."

Glaus, despite his "campus hunk" looks, was a very shy fellow who was not comfortable giving interviews.

Against New York he slammed three home runs in the '02 Divisional Series. His homer in Game 3 of the ALCS with Minnesota was a humdinger. He deposited an outside fastball from J.C. Romero over the right-field fence, the winning run in a tense 2–1 win.

"It was a great piece of hitting, going the other way," stated Twins catcher A.J. Pierzynski.

After capturing the Series MVP, Glaus told the media, "This is why we put all the time and effort in. All the swings against a garage door when you were a kid."

In a Fall Classic that at first focused all the attention on the incredible Barry Bonds, it was Glaus with his .385 average (10-for-26), three doubles, three homers, and eight runs batted in that stood tallest in the end.

"At this point, I don't even really know how I'm feeling except ecstatic," he said after the 4–1, seventh-game triumph.

"I was just so excited about being world champion. I didn't even really know what to think. These fans have been waiting a long time for this. And I know we're all happy to be part of the team to bring it to them...Actually, we've had that way of thinking all year. No matter what we came up against, we were going to play hard and leave it all out there, and that's what we did here."

TRIVIA

Where did Troy Glaus play college ball?

Answers to the trivia questions are on pages 189–190.

Glaus homered in the Game 1 4–3 loss to San Francisco, as well. It was his two-run double off fireballer Robb Nen in the eighth inning of the unreal sixth game that propelled the team all the way back from a 5–0 deficit to a 6–5 win, which ultimately sucked all the life out of the Giants.

"I think the feeling would be tremendous no matter where we were," he said, "but for me to be home, my friends and family to be here. They've all been a part of it. For them to be watching, and the fan support and everything—unbelievable."

Seventh Heaven

The 2002 World Series featured two teams with a past. Both managers, Mike Scioscia and Dusty Baker of the San Francisco Giants, were old Dodgers, of all things. They had shared the 1981 world championship together.

Barry Bonds of the Giants had never been to the World Series. He was finishing what may have been his greatest season. He had not hit 73 homers, as he had done in 2001, but he led the National League in batting average at .370. His combination of power, on-base percentage, bases on balls, and altered opposition strategy was unlike anything seen before. Only Babe Ruth in the 1920s had affected the game the way Bonds was. He was virtually unstoppable, a force above anything almost anybody alive had ever seen. He was in the second of what would be four straight MVP seasons. He had not yet sullied his reputation with steroid use, and at that point the question of whether he was the greatest baseball player in history seemed to be one that favored him.

But Bonds, always a star-crossed character, had been to the playoffs in the past and come up short. As a member of the Pirates, his off-line throw had allowed Atlanta to win the deciding game in 1992. He had gone into slumps at just the wrong time. People questioned his heart. But in the National League postseason, he carried San Francisco. He was hot, and few figured that he was going to stop himself.

The Anaheim pitching staff, in assessing Bonds, might well have recalled the words of Winston Churchill when he put Dwight Eisenhower in charge of D-day: "God himself must tremble at the task before you."

Mike Scioscia holds the 2002 World Series trophy as he rides on a float with vice president and general manager Bill Stoneman and Angels players in Anaheim in October 2002. Joining Scioscia and Stoneman is Series MVP Troy Glaus, standing next to Mickey Mouse.

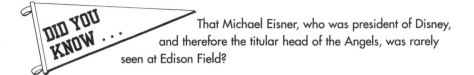
DID YOU KNOW . . . That Michael Eisner, who was president of Disney, and therefore the titular head of the Angels, was rarely seen at Edison Field?

The Giants also had history to contend with. Like the Angels, they had labored in the shadow of the Dodgers and the successful cross-bay A's. Since coming to the West Coast in 1958, Los Angeles and Oakland had won nine world championships between them. The Giants had won the same number as the Halos: zero.

They had been to the Fall Classic in 1962 (seven-game loss to the Yankees) and 1989 (four-game sweep to Oakland with an earthquake thrown in for good measure). Their postseason record was desultory. Once a baseball empire, they had not tasted the fruits of victory since 1954 at the Polo Grounds.

Two also-rans whose rivals were more successful organizations. In the Bay Area, everybody had won it except for San Francisco. In addition to the A's, the 49ers, the Raiders, and the Warriors had captured the brass ring. Even Cal and Stanford had won national titles in football once upon a time.

It also featured an all-California Series; not the first one, but the first between these two teams.

Anaheim lucked out with home-field advantage, but they were full of anxiety. They had weathered the storms of an Oakland 20-game winning streak, the almighty Yankees, the Metrodome, but the obstacle called Barry Bonds stood as tall as the Golden Gate Bridge.

The old Hollywood glitz descended upon Edison Field, just as they had at Dodger Stadium so many times, half an hour up the freeway. Charlie Sheen, a big Angels fan who once bought every left-field bleacher ticket so he and his private pals could have a free shot at home-run balls, was there with bells on.

So was Bonds, who went *deep* to key his club's 4–3 victory.

Game 2 was one for the history books. Like the second game of the playoffs at Yankee Stadium, Anaheim demonstrated why they were a team of destiny. Bonds hit another home run and scored three runs, so if they were to find a way to win, it would have to be some way other than by stopping him.

The Angels clobbered Russ Ortiz, connecting on their first 15 swings against him to take a 5–0 first-inning lead. Then San Francisco came right back with four runs. All the air was seemingly taken out of the Angels tires. The Rally Monkeys fell silent.

This was a heavyweight knockout contest. The Angels came back with two in the second, but their great middle relievers could not stem the Giants attack. San Francisco scored four times in the fifth, and their 9–7 lead might have been the last straw. Not this time. Not this game or this team. Not this year.

Rodriguez and Percival did one of the toughest jobs in baseball: closing the door on a hot team with the game on the line. The veteran Salmon seemed to be telling the world that Bonds was not the only star on the field. He went 4-for-4 with a walk, drove in four, and scored three. His homer capped the Angels comeback to equal all comebacks in an 11–10 win that, considering the Series shifted to San Francisco, was a must-win game.

After two games in sunny Southern California, the beach vibe gave way to cable car sophistication. San Francisco, a town that had once been ready to give up on baseball, was mad for their team. Bonds had certainly revived interest when a new ownership group saved the Giants then signed him to what was at the time the largest free-agent contract in the game's history.

But the beautiful stadium—pick a name: Pac Bell, SBC, and AT&T—had done more to make the Giants successful than any other factor. Now it was the center of the diamond universe.

The Angels avoided Barry Bonds as much as possible, walking him when they could, but he still went deep with two runs batted in. But offensively, the Angels were relentless at the plate and on the bases.

Scott Spiezio drove in three runs, Erstad had three hits, and Livan "I never lose in October" Hernandez gave up six runs in three and two-thirds innings, taking the 10–4 loss.

"Everybody knows that one run isn't enough, two runs aren't enough," Spiezio said. "No matter how many runs we score, we're going to go up there and act like that's the biggest at-bat we've ever had."

With the Angels, nobody expected it to be easy. Instead of taking a 3–1 lead with a chance to close it out at Pac Bell, the Angels fell,

TOP 10

Greatest California Major League Teams

	Year	Team
1.	1989	Oakland A's
2.	1974	Oakland A's
3.	1963	Los Angeles Dodgers
4.	1972	Oakland A's
5.	1965	Los Angeles Dodgers
6.	2002	Anaheim Angels
7.	1973	Oakland A's
8.	1988	Los Angeles Dodgers
9.	1988	Oakland A's
10.	1962	San Francisco Giants

4–3, with Francisco Rodriguez proving he was human in taking the loss. There was a sense of the old Angels folderoo: a 3–0 lead blown, a tie game in the bottom of the eighth on the road, and a defeat.

The next night the Angels' world fell apart. Bonds put on a hitting exhibition, going 3-for-4. His RBI double sent San Francisco into a big early lead. Jeff Kent sealed it with a pair of two-run home runs, and the big crowd just went berserk after that. When Rich Aurilia hit a three-run homer in the eighth, it gave the Giants the most runs, 16, in any Series game since New York beat Pittsburgh in 1960, 16–3.

The only consolation was that the teams were returning to the Southland, but the prospect of still another Angels disaster loomed like the Hindenburg over a New Jersey pasture. Russ Ortiz and Kevin Appier squared away, the tension thick enough to cut with a knife until the fifth when San Francisco touched the veteran right-hander for three runs, followed by one in the sixth and another in the seventh off Rodriguez, finally showing the pressure.

Trailing 5–0 in the bottom of the seventh, Anaheim finally got to Ortiz when Glaus and Fullmer made back-to-back singles. Baker came out for Ortiz, allowing him to leave the field with the game ball, as if to say victory was secure. The crowd, the Angels dugout, and the TV audience all saw it. Big mistake.

After three runs were in on the strength of Spiezio's three-run jack off Felix Rodriguez, the Giants were rattled. Clinging to a 5–3 lead in the eighth, with the Rally Monkeys and Thunder Sticks in full force, San Francisco was now doing what John Wooden always told his UCLA Bruins *never* to do: playing not to *win*, but rather playing *not to lose*. Anaheim came on again. Erstad homered to narrow the lead to one. After the Angels put a couple men on, Bonds made an error, and with closer Robb Nen called on to stem the tide, Glaus's two-run double gave Anaheim the 6–5 lead. Percival was "lights out" in the ninth. Now the season hung on a single game, with a "giant" switch of momentum in favor of the Halos.

When all was said and done, Bonds was not the difference. Like the Soviet and U.S. fleets meeting at sea during the Cuban Missile Crisis, the "other fellow blinked" as Dean

TRIVIA

How many other wild card teams have won the World Series?

Answers to the trivia questions are on pages 189–190.

Acheson famously remarked of the Russians. The "other fellow" in this case was San Francisco, who failed to deliver the last, best hope of their past 40 years since losing Game 7 of the '62 Classic to the Yanks, 1–0.

After all the offense, the comebacks, and the heroics, it was John Lackey, followed by bullpen aces Brendan Donnelly, Rodriguez, and Percival in a workmanlike 4–1 victory.

"You want the results to be different," said Bonds, who was 1-for-3 with no RBIs. "They outplayed us, they deserve it. They beat us. They're world champions."

Had the results been different, Bonds, not Glaus, would have been the Series Most Valuable Player.

"Somewhere, Gene Autry is smiling right now," said Commissioner Bud Selig.

ANGELS ESSENTIAL

Vlad the Impaler

Vladimir Guerrero put together two of the best offensive seasons of any Angels player, both of which led to division titles. He was voted the American League MVP in 2004, only the second Angel to receive that honor. He was a Triple Crown threat well into August. Perhaps Guerrero's greatest contribution has been his ability to help transform the Angels into a consistent winner.

Guerrero has not gone into protracted slumps, and therefore his team has not. The old Angels template was to have an occasional good season, and as if expending all energies in so doing, fall drastically in subsequent years. That appeared to be their destiny in 2003, when great expectation met disappointment, again.

But Guerrero has turned the Angels into consistent contenders. Entering 2006, he had not led them back to the Promised Land, but he did help edge his team higher (although the A's finished first in 2006, ahead of the Angels). Certainly, the 2000s now saw a true on-field rivalry between Oakland and the Angels at last.

In the final week of the 2004 season, he earned the MVP award via a crucial seven-game stretch in which he belted six home runs. Unfortunately, Guerrero did not match the accomplishments of Salmon or Glaus in his postseason work. The club, now occupying either a favorite's role, or at least not that of an underdog, managed to go silent. Guerrero hit a key grand slam in the '04 playoffs, but it was not enough.

Guerrero was well-regarded as one of the best players in base-ball but labored in obscurity in Montreal before coming to the high-profile Angels and the L.A. media glare. As an Angel his single-season accomplishments include batting .337 in 2004 with a .598

180

25—The number of Most Valuable Player Awards won by players on West Coast teams. They include:

Player	Team	Years
Maury Wills	Dodgers	1962
Sandy Koufax	Dodgers	1963
Willie Mays	Giants	1965
Willie McCovey	Giants	1969
Vida Blue	A's	1971
Reggie Jackson	A's	1973
Steve Garvey	Dodgers	1974
Don Baylor	Angels	1979
Jose Canseco	A's	1988
Kirk Gibson	Dodgers	1988
Kevin Mitchell	Giants	1989
Rickey Henderson	A's	1990
Dennis Eckersley	A's	1992
Barry Bonds	Giants	1993, 2001, 2002, 2003, 2004
Ken Caminiti	Padres	1996
Ken Griffey Jr.	Mariners	1997
Jeff Kent	Giants	2000
Jason Giambi	A's	2000
Ichiro Suzuki	Mariners	2001
Miguel Tejada	A's	2002
Vladimir Guerrero	Angels	2004

slugging percentage followed by .565 in '05. He scored 124 runs in 2004 with 206 hits, 366 total bases, 39 doubles, 39 homers, and 126 RBIs. Guerrero was issued 40 intentional walks as an Angel entering 2006. (Reggie Jackson had 47 in almost 1,500 more Angels at-bats.)

As a kid, he almost became a Dodger. They had the chance to sign him but went for his brother, Wilton, instead. Wilton became a reserve player. Montreal signed Vladimir at age 17. He debuted in the major leagues in 1996, reaching for the stars in 1997, when he hit .302.

Vladimir Guerrero hits a solo homer against the Seattle Mariners during his 2004 MVP season.

DID YOU KNOW ... That when the Angels were still at Dodger Stadium, Gene Autry entertained an offer from the city of Long Beach to build a stadium there under the proviso that the team be called the Long Beach Angels? Anaheim originally offered no objection to the team being called the California Angels, since the city received recognition on every news dateline and TV broadcast. It was not until the Disney transaction that the city insisted on having its name be used. Arte Moreno wisely changed the name back to the Los Angeles Angels, although he was forced to put "of Anaheim" in there to fulfill the contract with the city. Moreno recognized the broader market share of the club. Long Beach, for instance, is in L.A. County, but is often considered an Orange County demographic. Much of the San Gabriel Valley and the Inland Empire tend to Angels allegiance because of freeway proximity to Anaheim, even though they are not in Orange County. Growth in Riverside and San Bernardino, fairly easy commutes down the 91 Freeway, has created a natural Angels fan base.

Guerrero batted .300 or better every single year, reliably hitting 30-plus home runs a season (save for 2003, when back injuries limited him to 112 games). He appeared in all but one All-Star Game as an Expo (2003) since 1999. He earned the Silver Slugger award and was the hottest free agent in the 2003 off-season.

The Dodgers probably would have signed him, but the Frank McCourt purchase from Fox was ongoing, creating questions that ultimately prevented him from going to Los Angeles. Then the Angels stepped up in January 2004, signing Vlad to a five-year, $70 million deal.

With Oakland playing at Anaheim, two games ahead in the 2004 A.L. West race, Vlad hit .536 over the last seven games of the season, carrying his club on the road. Anaheim surpassed Oakland in the standings, beating the A's on their home turf to win the division. He only hit .167 against Boston pitching in the playoffs, though. In 2005 he had a shoulder injury that held him back in the playoffs.

Respect for History

"Arte Moreno wants to win and he wants to make money," wrote Rev Halofan, an obvious pen name for a blogger on www.halosheaven.com. "After years of the franchise being treated as Jackie Autry's medium-market and Michael Eisner's corporate synergy black sheep, it is good to have a visionary marketing genius who understands investing for long-term gains and short-term thrills."

Arte Moreno was not the owner of the club the year they won the 2002 World Series, but his greatest contribution has been keeping them in contention in the years since. In fickle L.A., he has effectively maintained the franchise as the marquee team in the Southland, a mighty accomplishment that Autry was never able to realize.

He "might be the best thing to ever happen to this franchise," wrote Rev Halofan.

Moreno's decision to rename the club the "Los Angeles Angels of Anaheim" has had mixed results. The "of Anaheim" appellation is ridiculous, but apparently necessary to ward off lawsuits as it technically fulfills the club's Disney contract with the city. There is precedent for naming a team that does not play in a city after that city. The New York Jets and Giants both play in New Jersey. The Detroit Pistons do not play in Detroit.

The desire to name the team after Anaheim or Orange County is a provincial one, even if relatively popular in the county. The fact is that Greater Los Angeles, Metropolitan L.A., the L.A. Basin, or the Southland—whatever term is applied—generally consists of a geographical range stretching between Ventura in the northwest; San Fernando in the north; Riverside and San Bernardino in the east; Malibu, Santa Monica, the South Bay, Palos Verdes

Estates, Long Beach, and Newport Beach in the west; and San Clemente in the south.

This is an area stretching roughly 100 to 120 miles north and south, and 60 to 90 miles east and west. It is connected by the 405, the 101, the 5, the 110, the 10, the 91, and the 605; traversing Orange, L.A., Ventura, Riverside, and San Bernardino Counties. It includes the 213, the 310, the 818, the 323, the 626, the 562, the 714, the 909, the 949, and several other area codes.

What is *not* Greater Los Angeles? Bakersfield and Kern County are not L.A. Neither is Santa Barbara, Edwards Air Force Base, Palm Springs, Big Bear, Oceanside, San Diego, or Catalina Island, although marketers and college recruiters from USC and UCLA might beg to differ. *Southern California* is not L.A. Southern California is everything south of Fresno and San Luis Obispo; all the deserts leading to Las Vegas, Arizona, and Mexico; San Diego, city and county; and the offshore islands from the Channels to Catalina.

Arturo "Arte" Moreno, who took over the Angels in 2003, is the first Latino owner of an American-based professional sports team.

All–Time
Angels

Position	Name
Right-Handed Pitcher	Nolan Ryan
Right-Handed Pitcher	Dean Chance
Left-Handed Pitcher	Chuck Finley
Left-Handed Pitcher	Frank Tanana
Left-Handed Pitcher	Mark Langston
Left-Handed Pitcher	Jim Abbott
Relief Pitcher	Troy Percival
Relief Pitcher	Francisco Rodriguez
Relief Pitcher	Minnie Rojas
Catcher	Bob Boone
Catcher	Buck Rodgers
First Baseman	Rod Carew
First Baseman	Wally Joyner
Second Baseman	Bobby Grich
Second Baseman	Bobby Knoop
Third Baseman	Troy Glaus
Shortstop	Jim Fregosi
Outfielder	Tim Salmon
Outfielder	Darin Erstad
Outfielder	Vladimir Guerrero
Designated Hitter	Reggie Jackson
Designated Hitter	Don Baylor
Manager	Mike Scioscia
Manager	Gene Mauch
Manager	Bill Rigney

For a baseball franchise prominently featured in newspapers, news broadcasts, TV, radio, and within the advertising sphere of all these disparate communities, to limit its identification to what amounts to only part of this "empire" made no sense to Moreno. He was right to think along these lines.

When people from most of these communities venture to other countries, or even to other parts of the U.S., and are asked where they hail from, they often reply, "L.A." or "near L.A." or "the L.A. area." Some might say "Orange County" or "Anaheim" or "Newport Beach," but as often as not further identification might then include "south of L.A." People driving on Interstate 5 on the way to Tustin, when asked where they are headed, might respond "L.A." to make it easy. This is similar to people from, say, Marin County who, when asked on a trip where they are from, say "San Francisco," or someone from Independence, Missouri, responding "Kansas City."

Arturo "Arte" Moreno grew up in a two-bedroom home in Tucson, Arizona. The oldest of 11 children, he took over the family-run *El Tucsonense* newspaper until it ceased publication in 1966. He worked for and continues to own the parallel family printing business, *Old Pueblo Printers*. He enlisted in the Army during Vietnam, serving in Indochina. Upon his return, he enrolled at the University of Arizona, where he graduated in 1973 with a Bachelor of Science degree in marketing. He has remained a Wildcats supporter.

Moreno sold billboard ads for Eller Outdoor, a Phoenix-based advertiser owned by Karl Eller, who "would become Moreno's mentor, boss, competitor, and, eventually, his neighbor and bitter enemy." Joining Outdoor Systems in 1984, Moreno eventually became president and CEO, parlaying the Phoenix-based billboard company into a national player, making it the largest space-advertising firm in the country, principally by buying smaller companies. Selling Outdoor Systems to Infinity/CBS in 1999 netted him around $960 million from a $8.7 billion sale, instantly making him one of the country's richest men.

Always a baseball fan and youth league coach, in 1986 he bought the Salt Lake City Trappers, a rookie league team. He worked the ticket booth, let kids in for free who wore Little League jerseys to the games, and was part of the wave of minor league entrepreneurs who turned many franchises into financial successes over the past 20 years.

"For some of the other guys, it was a toy," recalled former Trappers general manager Steve Pearson. "But for Arte, he always saw it as a business."

Moreno helped found the Arizona Diamondbacks but was unable to buy out the other investors in 2001, entering into a period of disagreement with his partners.

"I understand that when [D'backs owner] Jerry [Colangelo] said he was looking for additional money for the team, [Moreno] pulled out a sizable check and said, 'You don't need those investors. Here's my money'," recalled Jose Canchola, one of the original owners of the Trappers and a subsequent Diamondbacks investor.

Moreno was bought out but remained a part owner of the Phoenix Suns and in subsequent years patched up his relationship with Colangelo. When Disney desperately wanted to get rid of the Angels, Moreno was the right man at the right time. He reduced draft beer prices at Angels Stadium. He presided over two of the team's most productive—and expensive—off-seasons in its history, signing Vlad Guerrero, Bartolo Colon, Kelvim Escobar, Steve Finley, and Orlando Cabrera.

"Losing makes me puke," he once said.

Considered a "man's man," Moreno has successfully straddled the important white, middle-class community that has always anchored the Angels fan base, while tapping into the growing power of Hispanic market share. A self-made entrepreneur, a Vietnam vet, and an example of the American Dream, Moreno is a poster boy for Republican politics in the eyes of his Orange County constituency.

Moreno smartly dipped into club history, paying respect to it. That was at the heart of his decision to change the name back to the L.A. Angels. He also has paid homage to past Angels stars, and with the team's recent success has plenty of stars and history to pay homage to.

ANSWERS TO
TRIVIA QUESTIONS

Page 9: The San Diego Padres, Hollywood Stars, Los Angeles Angels, San Francisco Seals, Mission Reds, Oakland Oaks, Sacramento Solons, Portland Beavers, and Seattle Rainers made up the core of the Pacific Coast League.

Page 15: Bob Case was the Angels' clubhouse attendant when the team played at Dodger Stadium. He remained close friends with most of the old Angels and eventually came to own one of the best baseball memorabilia collections in the nation.

Page 30: The Coconut Grove was located in the Ambassador Hotel, located in the mid-Wilshire District.

Page 35: Leon "Daddy Wags" Wagner was the MVP of the second 1962 All-Star Game. For two years (1961–1962), baseball held two midsummer classics, one in each league's city. In 1962 the Nationals won 3–1 in Washington, D.C. The second game was played at Chicago's Wrigley Field. Wagner's homer propelled the AL to the 9–4 win.

Page 51: The first All-Star Game was played in Anaheim in 1967. Dean Chance started his second All-Star Game against San Francisco's Juan Marichal, and 30 All-Stars struck out. Jim McGlothlin of California pitched the fourth and fifth innings. Tony Perez of Cincinnati hit a game-winning home run in the fifteenth inning to give Don Drysdale the 2-1 win. The save went to Tom Seaver of the New York Mets, a rookie one year removed from the USC campus.

Page 54: Of Angel pitchers compiling more than 75 decisions and 500 innings pitched, Andy Messersmith has the lowest ERA.

Page 61: The powerful American League East featured Baltimore, Detroit, and Boston, all league champions in the previous three years. The American League West was weak for three seasons. Both expansion teams (Seattle and Kansas City) were placed in the division. Champions Minnesota and Oakland were a combined 0–9 versus Baltimore in the 1969–1971 ALCS.

Page 64: The one bright spot in 1971 was pitcher Andy Messersmith, who won 20 games with a 2.99 ERA.

Page 76: The term "Ryan Express" came from the 1965 Frank Sinatra film *Von Ryan's Express.*

Page 83: Talk of an "Angels Curse" started in 1977 when, in January of that year, promising Angels infielder Mike Miley was killed in an auto accident near his Louisiana home. Added to Minnie Rojas's paralyzing car crash and the Alex Johnson-Chico Ruiz gun incident, people began to question whether a curse befell the team. The Angels curse grew over the next two decades, with Frank Tanana's arm injury, Lyman Bostock's murder, defeat-from-the-jaws-of-victory in 1982 and 1986, the New Jersey bus crash in 1992, the '95 folderoo, and Tony Philips's arrest in a crack motel in 1997.

Page 89: The Angels celebrated the 1979 American League West championship at

Richard Nixon's San Clemente estate, which sat on a bluff overlooking the Pacific Ocean in southern Orange County.

Page 95: General Manager Dick Walsh was nicknamed "the Smiling Python" in part because he smiled while stabbing players in the back. For example, according to writer Ross Newhan, if he was not satisfied with the progress of a player's contract negotiations, he would write "poison pen letters" to the player's wives, informing them that their husbands were cheating on them on road trips. Needless to say, he was not popular.

Page 98: Bob Boone holds the unique role of being in the middle of one of the few grandfather-father-grandson(s) team ever to play in the big leagues. Grandfather Ray Boone came out of San Diego and was an All-Star third baseman at Cleveland. Bob starred for Philadelphia and California before becoming a manager. Two of his sons reached the majors—Bret starred for Seattle, and Aaron's 2003 playoff homer to beat Boston is one of the most memorable moments in Yankees history.

Page 104: The four ex-Most Valuable Players on the 1982 Angels were Reggie Jackson (1973), Fred Lynn (1975), Rod Carew (1977), and Don Baylor (1979).

Page 109: Tom Seaver won his 300th career game, defeating New York at Yankee Stadium, on August 4, 1985, the day Rod Carew collected his 3,000th career hit.

Page 118: Reggie Jackson first got into trouble in New York when he told a *SPORT* magazine writer that, "I'm the straw that stirs the drink. Thurman [Munson, the Yanks' All-Star catcher] can only stir it bad."

Page 126: George Sisler might be considered the best baseball player ever produced by the University of Michigan, aside from Jim Abbott. He was an All-American pitcher for the Wolverines under coach Branch Rickey. He later became a Hall of Fame first baseman under manager Branch Rickey with the St. Louis Browns.

Page 130: Leo "the Lip" Durocher roomed with Babe Ruth. Babe beat him up "within an inch of his life" for stealing his watch.

Page 141: Rex Hudler may very well be the single nicest guy in baseball. A prep superstar at Bullard High School in Fresno, Hudler turned down a football scholarship to Notre Dame, embarking on a 21-year (1978–1998) career in pro baseball. The ultimate journeyman, Hudler played for 18 different organizations (three years with the Angels) and one year in Japan. An Angels broadcaster, his style would be considered hokey except that it is genuinely the way the man is.

Page 145: Just before the 2000 season began, Jim "Hollywood" Edmonds was traded to St. Louis for Adam Kennedy and pitcher Kent Bottenfield.

Page 151: Darin Erstad was a punter on the 1994–1995 Nebraska Cornhuskers national championship teams.

Page 155: The 1994 film, *Angels in the Outfield,* starred Danny Glover and Joseph Gordon-Levitt in an endearing remake about a boy who has a chance to have a family if the Angels win the pennant. Actual angels answer his prayers to make his baseball and life dreams come true.

Page 161: The Rally Monkey is a miniature monkey replica made of fur and purchased at the stadium. It's kept away until the need to score runs materializes.

Page 173: Troy Glaus played college ball at UCLA.

Page 179: In addition to the 2002 Angels, three other wild card teams have won the World Series: Florida (1997 and 2003) and Boston (2004).

Los Angeles Angels All-Time Roster (through 2006 season)

A

Don Aase (P)	1978–84
Jim Abbott (P)	1989–92, 1995–96
Kyle Abbott (P)	1991, 1996
Shawn Abner (OF)	1991
Ricky Adams (SS)	1982–83
Joe Adcock (1B)	1964, 1965–66
Nick Adenhart (P)	2006
Willie Aikens (1B)	1977–79
Mike Aldrete (OF)	1995–96
Edgardo Alfonzo (3B)	2006
Luis Alicea (2B)	1997
Andy Allanson (C)	1995
Lloyd Allen (P)	1969–73
Bob Allietta (C)	1975
Sandy Alomar (2B)	1969, 1970–74
Juan Alvarez (P)	1999–2000
Orlando Alvarez (OF)	1976
Ruben Amaro (SS)	1969
Ruben Amaro (OF)	1991
Alfredo Amezaga (SS)	2002–04
Brian Anderson (P)	1993–95
Garret Anderson (OF)	1994–2006
Jim Anderson (SS)	1978–79
Kent Anderson (SS)	1989–90
Kevin Appier (P)	2002–03
Dan Ardell (1B)	1961
George Arias (3B)	1996, 1997
Tony Armas (OF)	1987–89
Jose Arredondo (P)	2006

Jason Aspito (OF)	2006
Ken Aspromonte (2B)	1961
David Austen (P)	2006
Earl Averill (C)	1961–62
Erick Aybar (SS)	2006
Joe Azcue (C)	1969, 1970–72

B

Stan Bahnsen (P)	1982
Scott Bailes (P)	1990–92
Ed Bailey (C)	1966
John Balaz (OF)	1974–75
Floyd Bannister (P)	1991
Steve Barber (P)	1972–73
Mike Barlow (P)	1977–79
Larry Barnes (1B)	2001
Jim Barr (P)	1979–80
Kimera Bartee (OF)	2000–01
Justin Baughman (2B)	1998, 2000
Don Baylor (DH)	1977–82
Chris Beasley (P)	1991
Julio Becquer (1B)	1961
Tim Belcher (P)	1998–2000
Bo Belinsky (P)	1962–64
Clay Bellinger (OF)	2002
Juan Beniquez (OF)	1981–85
Dennis Bennett (P)	1968
Erik Bennett (P)	1995
Dusty Bergman (P)	2004
Ken Berry (OF)	1971–73

Dante Bichette (OF)	1988–91	Bill Buckner (1B)	1987–1988
Mike Bielecki (P)	1995	Ryan Budde (C)	2006
Steve Bilko (1B)	1961–62	DeWayne Buice (P)	1987–88
Tim Bittner (P)	2006	Jason Bulger (P)	2006
Nate Bland (P)	2006	Lew Burdette (P)	1966–67
Steve Blateric (P)	1975	Tom Burgess (1B)	1962
Bert Blyleven (P)	1989–92	Tom Burgmeier (P)	1968
Bruce Bochte (1B)	1974–77	Jamie Burke (C)	2001
Frank Bolick (1B)	1998	Leo Burke (OF)	1961–62
Bobby Bonds (OF)	1976–77	Rick Burleson (SS)	1981–86
Bob Boone (C)	1982–88	Mike Butcher (P)	1992–95, 1998–99
Chris Bootcheck (P)	2003, 2005–06	Paul Byrd (P)	2005
Pedro Borbon (P)	1969		
Pat Borders (C)	1996	**C**	
Toby Borland (P)	2001	Orlando Cabrera (SS)	2005–06
Shawn Boskie (P)	1995–96	Greg Cadaret (P)	1997, 1998, 2000
Thad Bosley (OF)	1977, 1988	Mickey Callaway (P)	2002–03
Lyman Bostock (OF)	1978	Bert Campaneris (SS)	1979, 1980–81
Kent Bottenfield (P)	2000	John Candelaria (P)	1985, 1986–87
Ralph Botting (P)	1979–80	Tom Candiotti (P)	2000
Bob Botz (P)	1962	John Caneira (P)	1977–78
Peter Bourjos (C)	2006	Jose Cardenal (OF)	1965–67
Mike Bovee (P)	1997, 1998–99	Leo Cardenas (SS)	1972
Ted Bowsfield (P)	1961–62	Rod Carew (1B)	1979–85
Tom Bradley (P)	1969–70	Hector Carrasco (P)	2006
Brian Brady (OF)	1989	Jerry Casale (P)	1961
Ken Brett (P)	1977, 1978	Wayne Causey (SS)	1968
Jim Brewer (P)	1975–76	Bob Cerv (OF)	1961
Fritz Brickell (SS)	1961	Ray Chadwick (P)	1986
Rocky Bridges (SS)	1961	Dave Chalk (3B)	1973–78
Dan Briggs (1B)	1975–77	Bob Chance (1B)	1969
Bobby Brooks (OF)	1973	Dean Chance (P)	1961–66
Hubie Brooks (OF)	1992	Anthony Chavez (P)	1997
Scott Brow (P)	1998–99	Bruce Christensen (SS)	1971
Curt Brown (P)	1983	Jason Christiansen (P)	2005
Matthew Brown (3B)	2006	Archi Cianfrocco (1B)	2000
Mike Brown (OF)	1983–85, 1988	Pete Cimino (P)	1967–68
Randy Brown (C)	1969–70	Gino Cimoli (OF)	1965
Steve Brown (P)	1983–84	Bobby Clark (OF)	1979–83
Tom Brunansky (OF)	1981	Rickey Clark (P)	1967–72
George Brunet (P)	1964–69	Terry Clark (P)	1988–89
T.R. Bryden (P)	1986	Mark Clear (P)	1979–80, 1990

Edgard Clemente (OF)	2000
Pat Clements (P)	1985
Tex Clevenger (P)	1961
Stan Cliburn (C)	1980
Stu Cliburn (P)	1984–88
Lou Clinton (OF)	1964–65
Pete Coachman (3B)	1990
Jim Coates (P)	1965–67
Mike Colangelo (OF)	1999
Chris Coletta (OF)	1972
Dave Collins (OF)	1975–76
Michael Collins (1B)	2006
Bartolo Colon (P)	2004–06
Tony Conigliaro (OF)	1971
Billy Consolo (SS)	1962
Dennis Cook (P)	2002
Mike Cook (P)	1986–88
Bradley Coon (CF)	2006
Brian Cooper (P)	1999–2001
Doug Corbett (P)	1982–86
Sherman Corbett (P)	1988–90
Reid Cornelius (P)	1998–99
Rod Correia (SS)	1993–95
Chuck Cottier (2B)	1968–69
Marlan Coughtry (2B)	1962
Billy Cowan (OF)	1969–72
Al Cowens (OF)	1980
Terry Cox (P)	1970
Chuck Crim (P)	1992–93
Chris Cron (1B)	1991
Jim Crowell (P)	2006
Todd Cruz (SS)	1980
Mike Cuellar (P)	1977
John Cumberland (P)	1974
Chad Curtis (OF)	1992–95
John Curtis (P)	1982–84

D

John D'Acquisto (P)	1981
Paul Dade (OF)	1975–76
Mark Dalesandro (C)	1994–95
Bobby Darwin (OF)	1962

Vic Davalillo (OF)	1968–69
Jeff DaVanon (OF)	1999, 2001–05
Jerry Davanon (SS)	1973
Alvin Davis (1B)	1992
Bob Davis (C)	1981
Chili Davis (OF)	1988–90, 1993–96
Doug Davis (C)	1988
Mark Davis (OF)	1991
Tommy Davis (OF)	1976
Willie Davis (OF)	1979
Devin Day (2B)	2006
Doug DeCinces (3B)	1982–87
Steve Decker (C)	1999
Charlie Dees (1B)	1963–65
Brent Del Chiaro (C)	2006
Wilson Delgado (SS)	2003
Rich DeLucia (P)	1997–98
Darrell Dent (—)	2001–02
Jason Dickson (P)	1996–2000
Frank Dimichele (P)	1988
Gary DiSarcina (SS)	1989–2000
Chuck Dobson (P)	1974–75
John Doherty (1B)	1974–75
Brendan Donnelly (P)	2002–06
Jim Donohue (P)	1961–62
Tom Donohue (C)	1979–80
John Dopson (P)	1994
Brian Dorsett (C)	1988
Jim Dorsey (P)	1980
Brian Downing (DH)	1978–90
Denny Doyle (2B)	1974, 1975
Paul Doyle (P)	1970, 1972
Dick Drago (P)	1976–77
Rob Ducey (OF)	1992
Tom Dukes (P)	1972
Bob Duliba (P)	1963–64
Courtney Duncan (P)	2003
Scott Dunn (P)	2004–06
Steve Dunning (P)	1976
Ryne Duren (P)	1961–62
Trent Durrington (2B)	1999–2000, 2003

E

Mike Easler (OF)	1976
Damion Easley (2B)	1992–96
David Eckstein (SS)	2001–04
Steve Eddy (P)	1979
Ken Edenfield (P)	1995–96
Jim Edmonds (OF)	1993–99
Robert Eenhoorn (2B)	1996–97
Dick Egan (P)	1966
Tom Egan (C)	1965–70, 1974–75
Mark Eichhorn (P)	1990–92, 1996
Robert Ellis (P)	1996
Sammy Ellis (P)	1968
Angelo Encarnacion (C)	1997
Jim Eppard (OF)	1987–89
Mike Epstein (1B)	1973–74
Darin Erstad (OF)	1996–2006
Kelvim Escobar (P)	2004–2006
Cam Esslinger (P)	2004
Andy Etchebarren (C)	1975–77
Seth Etherton (P)	2000
Terry Evans (RF)	2006
Mike Eylward (1B)	2006

F

Jorge Fabregas (C)	1994–97, 2000–02
Ron Fairly (1B)	1978
John Farrell (P)	1993–94
Sal Fasano (C)	2002
Junior Felix (OF)	1991–92
Joe Ferguson (C)	1981–83
Jose Fernandez (3B)	2001
Bob Ferris (P)	1979–80
Mike Fetters (P)	1989–91, 1998
Cecil Fielder (1B)	1998
Chone Figgins (OF)	2002–06
Ed Figueroa (P)	1974–75
Jack Fimple (C)	1987
Chuck Finley (P)	1986–99
Steve Finley (OF)	2005
Richard Fischer (P)	2003–04
Todd Fischer (P)	1986

Eddie Fisher (P)	1969–72
Mike Fitzgerald (C)	1992
Al Fitzmorris (P)	1978
Kevin Flora (OF)	1991–95
Gil Flores (OF)	1977
Hank Foiles (C)	1963–64
Tim Foli (SS)	1982–83
Dan Ford (OF)	1979–81
Ken Forsch (P)	1981–86
Terry Forster (P)	1986
Tim Fortugno (P)	1992
Alan Foster (P)	1972
Art Fowler (P)	1961–64
Alan Fowlkes (P)	1985
Paul Foytack (P)	1963–64
Willie Fraser (P)	1986–90
Jim Fregosi (SS)	1961–71
Steve Frey (P)	1992–93
Todd Frohwirth (P)	1996
Dave Frost (P)	1978–81
Cody Fuller (CF)	2006
Brad Fullmer (DH)	2002–03
Mike Fyhrie (P)	1999–2000

G

Len Gabrielson (OF)	1967
Gary Gaetti (3B)	1991–93
Andres Galarraga (1B)	2004
Al Gallagher (3B)	1973
Dave Gallagher (OF)	1991, 1995
Ron Gant (OF)	2000
Carlos Garcia (2B)	1998
Miguel Garcia (P)	1987
Ralph Garr (OF)	1979–80
Adrian Garrett (DH)	1975–76
Greg Garrett (P)	1970
Ned Garver (P)	1961
Aubrey Gatewood (P)	1963–65
Vern Geishert (P)	1969
Craig Gerber (SS)	1985
Derrick Gibson (OF)	2004
Benji Gil (SS)	2000–03

Bill Gilbreth (P)	1974	Mike Harkey (P)	1995
Troy Glaus (3B)	1998–2004	Larry Harlow (OF)	1979–81
Gary Glover (P)	2003	Brian Harper (C)	1979–81
Greg Gohr (P)	1996	Tommy Harper (OF)	1975
Dave Goltz (P)	1982–83	Bill Harrelson (P)	1968
Larry Gonzales (C)	1993	John Harris (1B)	1979–81
Rene Gonzales (3B)	1992–93, 1995	Pep Harris (P)	1996–98
Jose Gonzalez (OF)	1992	Paul Hartzell (P)	1976–78
Tony Gonzalez (OF)	1970–71	Bryan Harvey (P)	1987–92
Danny Goodwin (DH)	1975–78	Shigetoshi Hasegawa (P)	1997–2001
Nick Gorneault (RF)	2006	Andy Hassler (P)	1971–76, 1980, 1981–83
Julio Gotay (SS)	1965	Chris Hatcher (OF)	2000
Billy Grabarkewitz (3B)	1973	Hilly Hathaway (P)	1992–93
Joe Grahe (P)	1990–94	Ryan Hawblitzel (P)	1998–99
Eli Grba (P)	1961–63	Von Hayes (OF)	1992
Craig Grebeck (2B)	1997	Mike Heathcott (P)	2000
Lenny Green (OF)	1964	Bob Heffner (P)	1968
Steve Green (P)	2001	Bob Heise (SS)	1974
Todd Greene (C)	1995–99	Woodie Held (SS)	1967–68
Kevin Gregg (P)	2003–06	Russ Heman (P)	1961
Tom Gregorio (C)	2003, 2005	Bret Hemphill (C)	1999
Bobby Grich (2B)	1977–86	Rickey Henderson (OF)	1997
Doug Griffin (2B)	1970	George Hendrick (OF)	1985–88
Tom Griffin (P)	1978	Matt Hensley (P)	2004, 2006
Jason Grimsley (P)	1996	Jackie Hernandez (SS)	1965–66
Kevin Gross (P)	1997	Ed Herrmann (C)	1976
Kelly Gruber (3B)	1993	Jack Hiatt (C)	1964, 1972
Mark Gubicza (P)	1997	Jim Hibbs	1967
Mario Guerrero (SS)	1976–77	Jim Hicks (OF)	1969, 1970
Vladimir Guerrero (OF)	2004–06	Donnie Hill (2B)	1990–91
Jose Guillen (OF)	2004	Glenallen Hill (OF)	2001
		Ken Hill (P)	1997–2000
H		Brett Hinchliffe (P)	2000
John Habyan (P)	1995	Chuck Hinton (OF)	1968
Ed Halicki (P)	1980	Butch Hobson (3B)	1981
Jimmie Hall (OF)	1967–68	Chuck Hockenbery (P)	1975
Shane Halter (3B)	2004	Glenn Hoffman (SS)	1989
Jack Hamilton (P)	1967–68	Al Holland (P)	1985
Ken Hamlin (SS)	1961	Dave Hollins (3B)	1997–98
Ike Hampton (C)	1975–79	Mike Holtz (P)	1996–2001
Ryan Hancock (P)	1996	Mark Holzemer (P)	1993–96
Rich Hand (P)	1973	Doug Howard (1B)	1972–74

Jack Howell (3B)	1985–91, 1996–97	Mick Kelleher (SS)	1982
Rex Hudler (2B)	1994–96	Rich Kelley (—)	2001
Charlie Hudson (P)	1975	Pat Kelly (2B)	2000
Terry Humphrey (C)	1976–79	Bill Kelso (P)	1964, 1966–67
Ken Hunt (OF)	1961–63	Howie Kendrick (2B)	2006
Jeff Huson (SS)	1999	Adam Kennedy (2B)	2000
		Dave Kingman (OF)	1977
I		Bob Kipper (P)	1985
Maicer Izturis (3B)	2005–06	Ed Kirkpatrick (OF)	1962–68
		Don Kirkwood (P)	1974–77
J		Bruce Kison (P)	1980–84
Bo Jackson (OF)	1994	Ron Kline (P)	1961
Reggie Jackson (OF)	1982–86	Ted Kluszewski (1B)	1961
Ron Jackson (1B)	1975–78, 1982–84	Chris Knapp (P)	1978–80
Delvin James (P)	2005	Bobby Knoop (2B)	1964, 1965–69
Johnny James (P)	1961	Joe Koppe (SS)	1961–65
Mike James (P)	1995–98	Andy Kosco (OF)	1972
Marty Janzen (P)	2002	Frank Kostro (3B)	1963
Stan Javier (OF)	1993	Casey Kotchman (1B)	2004–06
Gregg Jefferies (1B)	1998	Ray Krawczyk (P)	1988
Jesse Jefferson (P)	1981	Chad Kreuter (C)	1997–98
Tommy John (P)	1982–85	Gil Kubski (OF)	1980
Keith Johns (2B)	1998–99	Fred Kuhaulua (P)	1977
Alex Johnson (OF)	1970–71	Art Kusnyer (C)	1971–73
Gary Johnson (OF)	2003		
Keith Johnson (1B)	2000	**L**	
Lou Johnson (OF)	1961, 1969	Bob Lacey (P)	1983
Mark Johnson (1B)	1998	John Lackey (P)	2002–06
Jay Johnstone (OF)	1966–70	Frank LaCorte (P)	1984
Bobby Jones (OF)	1976–77	Joe Lahoud (OF)	1974–76
Greg Jones (P)	2003, 2005–06	Ken Landreaux (OF)	1977–78
Ruppert Jones (OF)	1985–87	Dick Lange (P)	1972–75
Wally Joyner (1B)	1986–91, 2001	Mark Langston (P)	1990–97
Jeff Juden (P)	1998	Carney Lansford (3B)	1978–80
		Dave LaRoche (P)	1970–71, 1977–80
K		Fred Lasher (P)	1971
Scott Karl (P)	2000	Barry Latman (P)	1964–65
Curt Kaufman (P)	1984	Jack Lazorko (P)	1987–88
Greg Keagle (P)	2000	Josh Leblanc (LF)	2006
Steve Kealey (P)	1968–70	Bob Lee (P)	1964–66
Pat Keedy (3B)	1985	Corey Lee (P)	2005

Don Lee (P)	1962–65	Frank Malzone (3B)	1966
Mike Lee (P)	1963	Mike Marshall (OF)	1991
Gene Leek (3B)	1961–62	Norberto Martin (2B)	1998
Craig Lefferts (P)	1994	Alfredo Martinez (P)	1980–81
Phil Leftwich (P)	1993–96	Brett Martinez (C)	2006
Mark Leiter (P)	1994	Carlos Martinez (1B)	1995
Frank Leja (1B)	1962	Damon Mashore (OF)	1998
Dave Lemanczyk (P)	1980	Jeff Mathis (C)	2005–06
Al Levine (P)	1999–2002	Dave Matranga (2B)	2005
Scott Lewis (P)	1990–94	Gary Matthews (OF)	2006
Jim Leyritz (C)	1997	Carlos May (OF)	1977
Rufino Linares (OF)	1985	Darrell May (P)	1996–97
Jose Lind (2B)	1995	Rudy May (P)	1965–74
Doug Linton (P)	1993	Ken McBride (P)	1961–65
Winston Llenas (2B)	1968–75	Kirk McCaskill (P)	1985–91
Bobby Locke (P)	1967–68	Bob McClure (P)	1989–91
Skip Lockwood (P)	1974	Tom McCraw (1B)	1973–74
Kevin Lomon (P)	1998–99	Jack McDowell (P)	1998–99
Baltazar Lopez (1B)	2006	Chuck McElroy (P)	1996–97
Carlos Lopez (OF)	1976	Orlando McFarlane (C)	1967–68
Marcelino Lopez (P)	1965–67	Jim McGlothlin (P)	1965–69
Ramon Lopez (P)	1966	Byron McLaughlin (P)	1983
Andrew Lorraine (P)	1994–95	Mark McLemore (2B)	1986–90
Vance Lovelace (P)	1988–89	Ken McMullen (3B)	1970–72
Torey Lovullo (2B)	1993	Dallas McPherson (3B)	2004–06
Steve Lubratich (3B)	1981–83	Bill Melton (3B)	1976
Gary Lucas (P)	1986–87	Tommy Mendoza (P)	2006
Urbano Lugo (P)	1985–88	Paul Menhart (P)	1998–99
Mark Lukasiewicz (P)	2001–02	Rudy Meoli (SS)	1971–75
Matt Luke (OF)	1999	Kent Mercker (P)	2000
Keith Luuloa (SS)	2000	Lou Merloni (2B)	2005
Fred Lynn (OF)	1981–84	Andy Messersmith (P)	1968–72
Barry Lyons (C)	1991	Bob Meyer (P)	1964
		J.B. Miadich (P)	2001, 2003
M		Jason Middlebrook (P)	2004
Dave Machemer (2B)	1978	Mike Miley (SS)	1975–76
Tony Mack (P)	1985	Darrell Miller (C)	1984–88
Mike Magnante (P)	1999	Dyar Miller (P)	1977–79
Joe Magrane (P)	1993–94	Rick Miller (OF)	1978–80
Mickey Mahler (P)	1981–82	Don Mincher (1B)	1967–68
Jim Maloney (P)	1971	Greg Minton (P)	1987–90

Steve Mintz (P)	1999
Yoshitaka Mizuo (P)	2004
Ron Moeller (P)	1961–63
Bengie Molina (C)	1998–2005
Jose Molina (C)	2001–06
Raul Mondesi (OF)	2004
Sid Monge (P)	1975–77
John Montague (P)	1979–80
Willie Montanez (1B)	1966
Aurelio Monteagudo (P)	1973
Rich Monteleone (P)	1988–89, 1995–96
Balor Moore (P)	1977
Donnie Moore (P)	1985–88
Kendry Morales (1B)	2006
Billy Moran (2B)	1961–64
Angel Moreno (P)	1981–82
Jose Moreno (OF)	1982
Tom Morgan (P)	1961–63
John Morris (OF)	1992
Bubba Morton (OF)	1966–69
Dustin Moseley (P)	2006
Jerry Moses (C)	1971
Curt Motton (OF)	1972
Rance Mulliniks (3B)	1977–79
Tom Murphy (P)	1968–72
Tommy Murphy (OF)	2006
Eddie Murray (1B)	1997
Greg Myers (C)	1992–95

N

Mike Napoli (C)	2006
Jerry Narron (C)	1983–86
Julio Navarro (P)	1962–64
Gene Nelson (P)	1993
Mel Nelson (P)	1963
Morris Nettles (OF)	1974–75
Phil Nevin (3B)	1998
Fred Newman (P)	1962–67
Jerry Nielsen (P)	1993
Jose Nieves (SS)	2001–02
Junior Noboa (2B)	1988
Gary Nolan (P)	1977

Tim Nordbrook (SS)	1976
Joe Nuxhall (P)	1962

O

Mike O'Berry (C)	1983
Charlie O'Brien (C)	1998–99
Syd O'Brien (3B)	1971–72
Ken Oberkfell (3B)	1992
Alex Ochoa (OF)	2002
Kevin Ohme (P)	2004
Omar Olivares (P)	1998–99
Bob Oliver (1B)	1972–74
Phil Ortega (P)	1969
Ramon Ortiz (P)	1999–2004
John Orton (C)	1989–93
Dan Osinski (P)	1962–64
Ed Ott (C)	1981
Mike Overy (P)	1976
Spike Owen (SS)	1994–95
Eric Owens (OF)	2003
Ray Oyler (SS)	1970

P

Joe Pactwa (P)	1975
Matt Pali (LF)	2006
Orlando Palmeiro (OF)	1995–2002
Billy Parker (2B)	1971–73
Dave Parker (OF)	1991
Lance Parrish (C)	1989–92
Freddie Patek (SS)	1980–81
Bob Patterson (P)	1994–95
Ken Patterson (P)	1993–94
Marty Pattin (P)	1968
Josh Paul (C)	2004–05
Adam Pavkovich (3B)	2006
Albie Pearson (OF)	1961–66
Aaron Peel (RF)	2006
Orlando Pena (P)	1974–75
Brad Pennington (P)	1996
Joel Peralta (P)	2005
Troy Percival (P)	1995–2004
Eduardo Perez (1B)	1993–95

Marty Perez (SS)	1969–70	Rick Reichardt (OF)	1964–70
Matt Perisho (P)	1997	Jerry Remy (2B)	1975–77
Ron Perranoski (P)	1973	Steve Renko (P)	1981–82
Bob Perry (OF)	1963–64	Roger Repoz (OF)	1967–72
Mark Petkovsek (P)	1999–2000	Chris Resop (P)	2006
Dan Petry (P)	1988–89	Merv Rettenmund (OF)	1978–80
Gary Pettis (OF)	1982–87	Jerry Reuss (P)	1987
P.J. Phillips (SS)	2006	Ivan Reyes (2B)	2006
Tony Phillips (OF)	1995, 1997	Archie Reynolds (P)	1971
Rob Picciolo (SS)	1984	Harold Reynolds (2B)	1994
Ron Piche (P)	1965	Tommie Reynolds (OF)	1970–71
Jim Piersall (OF)	1963–67	Del Rice (C)	1961
Horacio Pina (P)	1974	Jeff Richardson (P)	1990
Vada Pinson (OF)	1972–73	Adam Riggs (2B)	2003–04
Gus Polidor (SS)	1985–88	Juan Rivera (OF)	2005–06
Luis Polonia (OF)	1990–93	Mickey Rivers (OF)	1970–75
Gregory Porter (3B)	2006	Rich Robertson (P)	1998
Lou Pote (P)	1999–2002	Don Robinson (P)	1992
Vic Power (1B)	1964–65	Frank Robinson (OF)	1973–74
Bob Priddy (P)	1969	Jeff Robinson (P)	1991
Curtis Pride (OF)	2004–06	Buck Rodgers (C)	1961–69
Chris Prieto (OF)	2005	Eric Rodland (2B)	2006
Bret Prinz (P)	2005	Aurelio Rodriguez (3B)	1967–70
Chris Pritchett (1B)	1996, 1998–99	Ellie Rodriguez (C)	1974–75
Aaron Pullin (P)	2006	Francisco Rodriguez (P)	2002–06
		Rich Rodriguez (P)	2003
Q		Sean Rodriguez (SS)	2006
Mel Queen (P)	1970–72	Minnie Rojas (P)	1966–68
Robb Quinlan (1B)	2003–06	Ron Romanick (P)	1984–86
Luis Quintana (P)	1974–75	J.C. Romero (P)	2006
		Phil Roof (C)	1965
R		Anderson Rosario (LF)	2006
Julio Ramirez (OF)	2002–03	Bobby Rose (2B)	1989–92
Orlando Ramirez (SS)	1974–79	Don Rose (P)	1972
Domingo Ramos (SS)	1988	Gary Ross (P)	1975–77
Merritt Ranew (C)	1965	Jonathon Rouwenhorst (P)	2006
Pat Rapp (P)	2001	Jorge Rubio (P)	1966–67
Doug Rau (P)	1981	Joe Rudi (OF)	1977–80
Johnny Ray (2B)	1987–90	Vern Ruhle (P)	1986
Barry Raziano (P)	1974	Chico Ruiz (2B)	1970–71
Joe Redfield (3B)	1988	Mark Ryal (OF)	1986–87
Howie Reed (P)	1966	Nolan Ryan (P)	1972–79

S

Bob Sadowski (3B)	1963
Ed Sadowski (C)	1961–63
Darrell Sales (RF)	2006
Tim Salmon (OF)	1992–2004, 2006
Bill Sampen (P)	1994
Luis Sanchez (P)	1981–85
Ken Sanders (P)	1974
Scott Sanderson (P)	1993, 1995–96
Charlie Sands (DH)	1973–74
Jack Sanford (P)	1965–67
Ervin Santana (P)	2005–06
Tom Satriano (C)	1961–69
Joe Saunders (P)	2005–06
Paul Schaal (3B)	1964–68, 1974
Richie Scheinblum (OF)	1973–74
Travis Schlichting (3B)	2005–06
Jeff Schmidt (P)	1996
Scott Schoeneweis (P)	1999–2003
Dick Schofield (SS)	1983–92, 1995–96
Bill Schroeder (C)	1989–90
Rick Schu (3B)	1990
Dave Schuler (P)	1979–80
Jeff Schwarz (P)	1994
Daryl Sconiers (1B)	1981–85
Darryl Scott (P)	1993
Mickey Scott (P)	1975–77
Aaron Sele (P)	2002–04
Dave Sells (P)	1972–75
Dick Selma (P)	1974
Ray Semproch (P)	1961
Alex Serrano (P)	2006
Harvey Shank (P)	1970
Andy Sheets (SS)	1999
Steven Shell (P)	2006
Larry Sherry (P)	1968
Scot Shields (P)	2001–06
Craig Shipley (3B)	1998
Costen Shockley (1B)	1965
Norm Siebern (1B)	1966
Tom Silverio (OF)	1970–72
Dave Silvestri (3B)	1999
Curt Simmons (P)	1967
Dick Simpson (OF)	1962–65
Wayne Simpson (P)	1977
Bill Singer (P)	1973–75
Dave Skaggs (C)	1980
Bill Skowron (1B)	1967
Jim Slaton (P)	1984–86
Don Slaught (C)	1996
Billy Smith (2B)	1975–76
Bobby Gene Smith (OF)	1965
Casey Smith (3B)	2006
Dave Smith (P)	1984–85
Dwight Smith (OF)	1994
Lee Smith (P)	1995–96
Stantrel Smith (2B)	2006
Willie Smith (OF)	1964–66
J.T. Snow (1B)	1993–96
Luis Sojo (2B)	1990–92
Tony Solaita (1B)	1976–78
Zach Sorensen (2B)	2005
Al Spangler (OF)	1965–66
Steve Sparks (P)	1998–99
Brian Specht (2B)	2006
Justin Speier (P)	2006
Jim Spencer (1B)	1968–73
Scott Spiezio (1B)	2000–03
Jack Spring (P)	1961–64
Dennis Springer (P)	1996–97
Russ Springer (P)	1993–95
Bob Sprout (P)	1961
Leroy Stanton (OF)	1972–76
Hainley Statia (2B)	2006
Rick Steirer (P)	1982–84
Rick Stelmaszek (C)	1973
John Stephenson (C)	1971–73
Lee Stevens (1B)	1990–93
Kurt Stillwell (SS)	1993
Kevin Stocker (SS)	2000
Bill Stoneman (P)	1974
Dick Stuart (1B)	1969
Moose Stubing	1967
Bill Sudakis (3B)	1975

LOS ANGELES ANGELS ALL-TIME ROSTER

Ed Sukla (P)	1964, 1965–66
Don Sutton (P)	1985, 1986–87
Craig Swan (P)	1984
Paul Swingle (P)	1993

T

Frank Tanana (P)	1973–80
Chuck Tanner (OF)	1961–62
Jarvis Tatum (OF)	1968–70
Ken Tatum (P)	1969–70
Hawk Taylor (C)	1967
Derrel Thomas (2B)	1984
George Thomas (OF)	1961–63
Lee Thomas (OF)	1961–64
Jason Thompson (1B)	1980
Dickie Thon (SS)	1979–80
Faye Throneberry (OF)	1961
Luis Tiant (P)	1982
Ron Tingley (C)	1989–93
Jeff Torborg (C)	1971–73
Felix Torres (3B)	1962–64
Rusty Torres (OF)	1976–77
Drew Toussaint (LF)	2006
Bill Travers (P)	1981–83
Bobby Trevino (OF)	1968
Mark Trumbo (1B)	2006
Bob Turley (P)	1963
Derrick Turnbow (P)	2000, 2003–04
Chris Turner (C)	1993–97
Ken Turner (P)	1967

U

Tim Unroe (1B)	1999

V

Ismael Valdez (P)	2001
Bobby Valentine (SS)	1973–75
Ellis Valentine (OF)	1983
Fernando Valenzuela (P)	1991
Julio Valera (P)	1992–93
Ben Van Ryn (P)	1996
Ty Vanburkleo (1B)	1993

Mo Vaughn (1B)	1999–2000
Randy Velarde (2B)	1996–99
Max Venable (OF)	1989–91
John Verhoeven (P)	1976–77
Charlie Vinson (1B)	1966
Bill Voss (OF)	1969–70

W

Leon Wagner (OF)	1961–63
Matt Walbeck (C)	1998–2000
Jim Walewander (2B)	1993
Chico Walker (OF)	1988
Tom Walker (P)	1977
Donne Wall (P)	2002
Don Wallace (2B)	1967
Tim Wallach (3B)	1996
Jerome Walton (OF)	1993
Dick Wantz (P)	1965
Bryan Ward (P)	2000
Jackie Warner (OF)	1966
Greg Washburn (P)	1969
Jarrod Washburn (P)	1998–2005
Claudell Washington (OF)	1989–90
Allen Watson (P)	1997–98
Mark Watson (P)	2005
Eric Weaver (P)	2000
Jeff Weaver (P)	2006
Jered Weaver (P)	2006
Jim Weaver (P)	1967–68
Ben Weber (P)	2000–04
Johnny Werhas (3B)	1967
Barry Wesson (OF)	2003
Gary Wheelock (P)	1976
Devon White (OF)	1985–90
Dan Whitmer (C)	1980
Rob Wilfong (2B)	1982, 1983–86
Hoyt Wilhelm (P)	1969
Nick Willhite (P)	1967
Mitch Williams (P)	1995
Reggie Williams (OF)	1992, 1998–2000
Shad Williams (P)	1996–97
Reggie Willits (OF)	2006

Terry Wilshusen (P)	1973	Clyde Wright (P)	1966–73
Bobby Wilson (C)	2006	Butch Wynegar (C)	1987–88
Tack Wilson (OF)	1987	Billy Wynne (P)	1971
Trevor Wilson (P)	1998		
Gordie Windhorn (OF)	1962	**Y**	
Dave Winfield (OF)	1990–91	Esteban Yan (P)	2005–06
Matt Wise (P)	2000–02	Eddie Yost (3B)	1961–62
George Witt (P)	1962	Cliff Young (P)	1990–91
Mike Witt (P)	1981–90		
Wally Wolf (P)	1969–70	**Z**	
Brandon Wood (SS)	2006	Geoff Zahn (P)	1981–85
Jake Woods (P)	2005	Pete Zamora (P)	2004
Shawn Wooten (1B)	2000–03	Bob Zimmerman (P)	2006

Notes

Little Big Man

He was "popular mainly because of my lack of size. I never heard a boo in my life. I was the hero for the guy who never made it..." Goldman, Robert, *Once They Were Angels*, Champaign, IL: Sports Publishing, 2006.

Satriano was very moved by the fact that Pearson was "super religious, he never said, 'damn' or 'hell' or anything like that..." Goldman, Robert, *Once They Were Angels*, Champaign, Il: Sports Publishing, 2006.

"So this one chick thought he was her date," said Belinsky. "Albie's real cute and she just falls in love with him..." Allen, Maury, *Bo" Pitching and Wooing*, New York: Dial Press, 1973.

The Big A

"I advise you to get out from under as soon as you can." Newhan, Ross, *The Anaheim Angels: A Complete History*, New York: Hyperion, 2000.

The New Breed

Wagner "got so that looking up, I really had the point of my nose on the ball all the way up and down." Walker, he said in 1962, "made me a Major League outfielder," but Walker's protests did not prevent Wagner from being lost to the Angels in the 1961 expansion shake-up. *1963 Official Baseball Almanac*, Greenwich, CT: Gold Medal Books, 1963.

Bill Rigney, who had turned down multi-year contracts ultimately worth $200,000 because "I don't want to leave the job undone with the

Angels" and "California's still my home," was fired. Newhan, Ross, *The Anaheim Angels: A Complete History*, New York: Hyperion, 2000.

The Ryan Express

"He was just blowing the ball by people," recalled Carew. Goldman, Robert, *Once They Were Angels*, Champaign, Il: Sports Publishing, 2006.

"Ryan was a more physical pitcher," said ex-Angel manager Norm Sherry, whose brother Larry was Koufax's teammate in L.A. Newhan, Ross, *The Anaheim Angels: A Complete History*, New York: Hyperion, 2000.

Lean Years

"I always felt our biggest competition was [Dodger broadcaster] Vin Scully," said general manager Buzzie Bavasi, a longtime Dodger executive before moving to Anaheim. Newhan, Ross, *The Anaheim Angels: A Complete History*, New York: Hyperion, 2000.

"Yes, We can!"

"He was the enforcer," Carew said of Baylor. Newhan, Ross, *The Anaheim Angels: A Complete History*, New York: Hyperion, 2000.

"I imagine he's 'bout as happy right now as he can remember being," Nolan Ryan observed of Autry. Newhan, Ross, *The Anaheim Angels: A Complete History*, New York: Hyperion, 2000.

Perennial All-Star

What set Fregosi apart, according to ex-teammate Eli Grba, was his "fire in the belly..." Goldman, Robert, *Once They Were Angels*, Champagne, Il.: Sports Publishing, 2006.

Reggie! Reggie!

"You'd sit down with Charlie," he once said, "and he'd say, 'Why, this man hit 15 fewer home runs than he had in this previous season,' or 'Why should I pay a man more to hit seven fewer homers' or 'he drove in 118 runs in 1969 and only 118 in 1973, why that's not improvement!' " Jackson, Reggie with Mike Lupica, *Reggie*, New York: Random House, 1984; also *SportsCentury*, Bristol, Ct: ESPN, 2000.

"The Grandest Gentleman in the Game."

"It broke me up; it broke my heart," said Reese. Bisheff, Steve, *Tales From the Angels Dugout*, Champaign, Il.: Sports Publishing, 2003.

Malaise

"You look at the Rams occupying this field, also," he said of a team considered football's best organization when they played at the L.A. Coliseum, then the worst when they played at the Big A, then a Super Bowl champion when they moved to St. Louis. "Maybe they were the smart ones by leaving." Newhan, Ross, *The Anaheim Angels: A Complete History*, New York: Hyperion, 2000.

"The Singing Cowboy"

"In the movies, I never lost a fight," he once said. Bisheff, Steve, *Tales From the Angels Dugout*, Champaign, Il.: Sports Publishing, 2003.

"I think what struck you about him," said Bobby Knoop, "is that for someone so successful and wealthy, he was such a kind and humble man." Bisheff, Steve, *Tales From the Angels Dugout*, Champaign, Il.: Sports Publishing, 2003.

Deliverance

"I've never been to the playoffs, but I can't imagine anything much more adrenaline-filled than this," said Percival after closing out the game. Beacham, Greg, "Pitching Duel Ends in Angels Victory," Associated Press, September 18, 2002.

"I had a glimpse of it my first year, but that has been a sour note in my career until now," Anderson said after the 10–5 win over Texas on September 26 clinched a postseason berth. Hawkins, Stephen, "Angels Clinch Playoff Berth, It's Party Time," Associated Press, September 27, 2002.

Mike Scioscia

"I remember playing sports my whole life," Scioscia said. Haakenson, Joe, *Out of the Blue*, Lincoln, NE: iUniverse, 2005.

"A recruiter said I was too small and too slow for guys at that level," he said. Travers, Steven, "Angels Hope to Fly," *StreetZebra*, June 2000.

Yankee Killers
"If they keep playing the way they're playing, no one is going to beat them," said Yankee shortstop Derek Jeter. Nadel, John, "Wooten, Molina and Gil Lead Angels Past New York Yankees," Associated Press, October 6, 2002.

Team of Destiny
"They're on a roll," Minnesota manager Ron Gardenhire said afterward. Nadel, John, "Kennedy's Three Homers Send Angels to Their First World Series," Associated Press, October 14, 2002.

The Quiet Man
"I always felt if you had a chance to stay in the same place your whole career, it would be something special," Salmon said of his decision to remain an Angel instead of signing with the hometown D'backs. Haakenson, Joe, *Out of the Blue*, Lincoln, NE: iUniverse, 2005.

"It's all so amazing, so unbelievable, I can't even begin to describe my emotions," Salmon said afterwards. Bisheff, Steve, *Tales From the Angels Dugout*, Champaign, Il.: Sports Publishing, 2003.

"It's been really sweet, especially since we've been close a few times, had some tough collapses," he said. *Anaheim Angels: World Series Champions*, Champaign, Il: Sports Publishing, 2002.

Hero
"Troy's ceiling is amazing," said Scioscia. "I think he has more upside than anybody else in this clubhouse." Bisheff, Steve, *Tales From the Angels Dugout*, Champaign, Il.: Sports Publishing, 2003.

"At this point, I don't even really know how I'm feeling except ecstatic," he said after the 4–1 seventh-game triumph. *Anaheim Angels: World Series Champions*, Champaign, Il: Sports Publishing, 2002.

"I think the feeling would be tremendous no matter where we were," he said, "but for me to be home, my friends and family to be here...unbelievable." Blum, Ronald, "Troy Glaus: World Series MVP," Associated Press, October 28, 2002.

Seventh Heaven
"Everybody knows that one run isn't enough, two runs aren't enough," Spiezio said. Walker, Ben, "Angels' Torrid Hitting Wins Game Three," Associated Press, October 23, 2002.

"You want the results to be different," said Bonds, who was one-for-three with no RBIs. Walker, Ben, "Angels in Seventh Heaven," Associated Press, October 28, 2002.

Respect for History
Moreno sold billboard ads for Eller Outdoor, a Phoenix-based advertiser owned by Karl Eller, who "would become Moreno's mentor, boss, competitor, and, eventually, his neighbor and bitter enemy." halosheaven.com

"I understand that when Jerry [D'backs owner Colangelo] said he was looking for additional money for the team, (Moreno) pulled out a sizable check and said, you don't need those investors. Here's my money," recalled Jose Canchola, one of the original owners of the Trappers and a subsequent Diamondbacks investor. halosheaven.com